CALUM FRANKLIN

THE MODERN PIE MAKER

A mouth-watering journey around Britain in eighty recipes

Photography by John Carey

BLOOMSBURY ABSOLUTE
LONDON • OXFORD • NEW YORK • NEW DELHI • SYDNEY

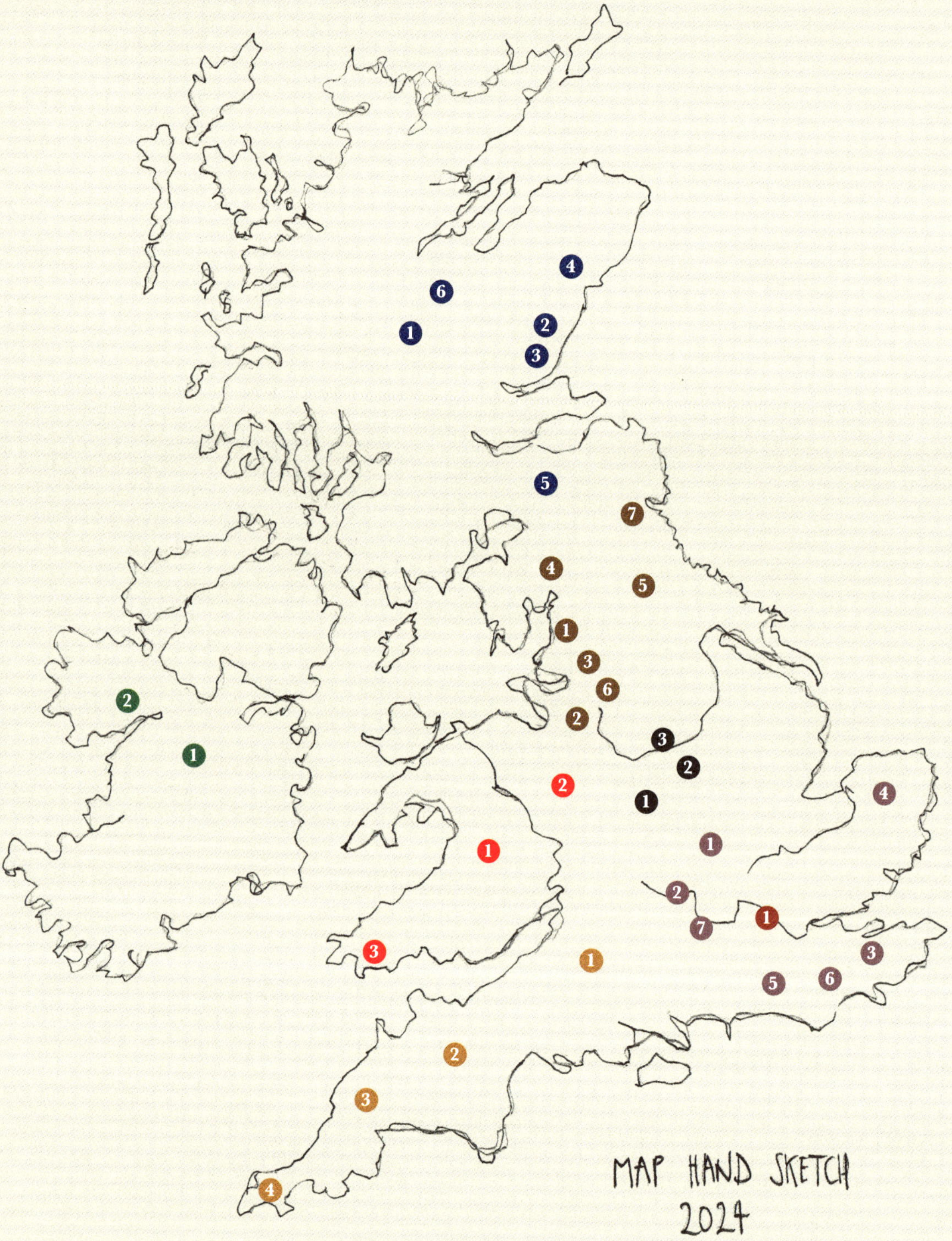
MAP HAND SKETCH
2024

Scotland

1.	Scotch Pies
2. Forfar *(nr Dundee)*	Forfar Bridies
3. Dundee	Macaroni Pies
4. Edzell	Mince and Skirlie Pies
5. Hawick	Teviotdale Pie
6. Moorlands	Bilberry Pies

London

1.	Beef and Oyster Pudding Quail Timbales Woolton Pie Mince and Cheese Pie Prawn Patties Figgy Pudding

North England

1. Preston	Butter Pie
2. Cheshire	Cheshire Pork Pie
3. Lancashire	Lancashire Foots Onion Pie
4. Kendal	Lobster Cannelons
5. Yorkshire	Yorkshire Christmas Pie
6. Manchester	Manchester Tart
7. Newcastle	Peppered Steak Slice

South West

1. Wiltshire	Wiltshire Lattice
2. Devon	Homity Pie
3. Cornwall	Cornish Pasty Hoggan Pies Likky Pie
4. Mousehole	Stargazy Pie

Midlands

1. Birmingham	Balti Pie
2. Melton Mowbray	Pork Pie Gala Pie Ploughman's Pork Pie
3. Mansfield	Mansfield Pie

Wales/borders

1.	Pastai Gocos Welsh Corned Beef Pie Welsh Oggie
2. Shropshire	Fidgit Pie
3. South Pembrokeshire	Katt Pies

South East

1. Bedfordshire	Bedfordshire Clanger
2. Buckinghamshire	Buckinghamshire Bacon Badger Rabbit Pie
3. Kent	Herb Pie Tail Pie
4. Norfolk	Norfolk Plough Pudding
5. Sussex	Sussex Pond Pudding Rasher Pudding
6. East Sussex	Banoffee Pie
7. Windsor	Apple Pie

Ireland

1.	Shepherd's Pie
2. Galway	Trawler Pie

It started with the Norfolk Plough Pudding and it ended with the Buckinghamshire Bacon Badger. In 2023 I started researching historical British pie recipes as part of the menu planning for a new restaurant opening. While delving into the archives I came across the Norfolk Plough Pudding, a dish that is steeped in British history and customs, dating all the way back to Tudor times. Despite all my years working in professional kitchens, running The Pie Room in central London and even being nicknamed 'The Pie King' by Jamie Oliver, I previously knew nothing at all about this pie, but it just grabbed me.

After spending some time reading more recipes, the next day I cooked my first Norfolk Plough Pudding. Or rather an attempt at it, which I posted on Instagram. Norfolk went wild. To start with, people gave me their constructive criticisms, which were useful, and everyone was very polite. But then they began to point out my inaccuracies amongst themselves… and they were slightly less polite. Then they started rowing amongst themselves. Then Suffolk got involved. Then Lincolnshire pitched in. The next morning, I was on BBC Norfolk discussing the heated debate that had resulted in this pie pile-on.

This book started that very day. I realised there is a tribal passion and pride for regional pies across Britain that I don't think occurs with any of our other national dishes, and I wanted the rest of the world to know about it. But while the inspiration for this book began that day in the British Library, we really should rewind a little further…

My background is as a chef with over 25 years of experience cooking in and running some of London's best restaurants. I studied classical fine dining, but then slowly moved towards a simpler style of ingredient-led British cookery in my thirties. In 2017, at the Holborn Dining Room, I created The Pie Room – a Victorian-style pie kitchen where we created and cooked traditional pies that were then sold directly to customers through a window onto the street. I designed The Pie Room purely to indulge my obsession with the craft of pie making and pastry work. Here, alongside a team of brilliant, passionate chefs, I pushed British pies to a level that garnered international interest.

Over a pretty short period of time, while we created pies in our little room on High Holborn, we found ourselves on TV shows around the world and on the pages of fashion magazines in Japan, France and the USA. Soon we were invited to cook alongside other chefs in their restaurants, to share our skills. I took our pies to Los Angeles, Copenhagen and Reykjavik, and demonstrated pastry techniques in Shanghai, Lagos and countless other cities. I wrote *The Pie Room*, my first cookbook that was published in 2020, which went on to become an award-winning bestseller and has been translated into many languages, helping to spread British pie making out to a wider audience.

Now, I am continuing on my quest to preserve and promote British pies, from the classic to the obscure. As I burrowed down into my research, I realised that many of the most interesting historical regional pies were in danger of extinction. Some pies had waned in popularity over time due to the nation's changing tastes or culinary fashions. Or perhaps there is now a general desire for a lighter touch with dough. I was worried that if I did manage to capture all of these pie recipes in a book, would people want to cook them all? It was at that point my aim for this book was cemented: I would research the origins and histories of these pies, as without exception they have all changed in one way or another over time, and then I would give my modern interpretation of each dish. To bring these pies up to date, I have deployed the cooking techniques that I have learned over the years, elevating and sometimes lightening the recipes to keep them relevant in hope that people will continue making them for years to come.

The Modern Pie Maker is my call to action to you, the reader and pie lover. Join me by playing your equally important role in preserving this unique part of British culinary heritage for future generations – and at the same time, you get to enjoy the most delicious-tasting and stunning-looking pies.

Now, if you had asked the slightly rebellious (sorry Mum) teenage Calum if he could imagine that in his forties he would be sitting in the British Library for weeks researching ancient British pies, getting excited at holding copies of nineteenth-century cookbooks, he would have laughed at you. But here we are, and I couldn't be happier.

The illustrations that you will see over the following pages are mine. I have included them where I felt the original design of the pie is helpful to see, to understand its roots and history. These sketches are also there to show, when alongside my updated recipes, how pie making has progressed with modern techniques and ingredients.

This project has taught me so much and continues to do so; pie making and recipes as a whole are artefacts – they reveal layers of social history and point to the wider culture of those times. Recipes are more than something to be enjoyed and shared, they are important historical documents, a link to our past, and their progression mirrors our own.

This book has truly been a passion project, which I hope illuminates a part of British food culture that needs a little candlelight flickering over it in the darkness. By cooking these recipes, we do that together.

Calum Franklin

London, 2026

TOOLS & TECH-NIQUES

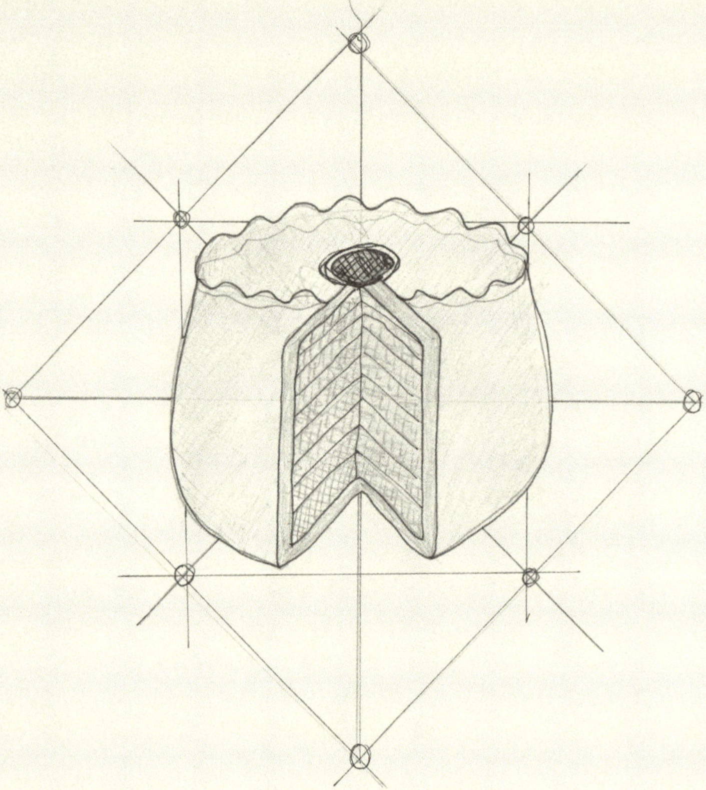

THE ANATOMY OF A PIE

I have long thought that the key to good pie making is, on a very basic level, giving equal consideration to what is outside as to what is inside. A pie should be as delicious to eat as it is appetising to look at; I have always strived for excellence on both counts. The reality is that there is so much to consider when building a pie: choosing the correct dough for the style of filling; creating and retaining any lamination in the dough as you work with it; rolling out the dough to the optimum thickness; adding any decoration to the exterior of the pie; deciding whether that decoration takes the form of crimping, cutting, scoring, plaiting or braiding; applying the necessary cooking time. I could go on. The techniques I set out below will help you understand and master these steps, then apply them to your own pie making.

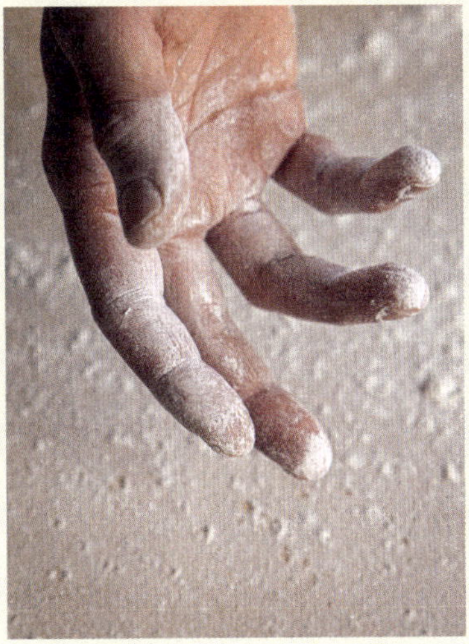

Making and handling dough

I cannot emphasise enough the importance of temperature when making and handling dough. By controlling the temperature of the dough and ensuring it is always cool enough to handle, you can use this to your advantage. At a cooler temperature, the dough itself stays supple for rolling, shaping, decorating, moving around and all the other things that end up being stressful when a dough is too warm. Temperature is also critical to achieving those all-important layers of lamination. If any dough becomes warm enough for the fat in it to melt, it will become homogeneous in texture. Puff pastry will not properly rise in those characteristic layers and shortcrust pastry will not have any separate flakes because the fat (usually butter) will have seeped all the way through the dough rather than staying as a distinct pocket ready to be activated at a high temperature in the oven.

To keep the fat inside the dough cool, always store your dough in the fridge until you are ready to use it. Keep a thick chopping board in the fridge, if you can, so when it is particularly warm in the kitchen, you can still roll or cut out your dough on a cold surface. Perhaps most importantly, afford yourself plenty of time. If at any point the dough becomes too soft, pop it back into the fridge for 15–20 minutes. (You can then use that down time for cleaning and organising your kitchen.) This really takes a lot of the stress out of pie making. Remember, pie making is important and anyone who tries to rush you really needs to have that communicated to them!

Chilling all your ingredients before starting a dough is one key to maintaining lamination. Cold fat, cold water, cold egg, etc. If your kitchen is really warm, you could even briefly chill the flour. However, only keep flour in the fridge for the maximum of one hour as it will start to absorb moisture and, when left too long, will eventually lead to a dampness that is unhelpful during sifting.

The basic method for rubbing in fats by hand is to pick up a little of the flour and fat mixture at a time and pass your thumb over your fingertips while letting the clumps fall back into the bowl. The quicker you are with this, the better the results will be as the fats stay cool. When rubbing the fat into the flour by hand, if you feel your hands are too hot, put on a pair of latex gloves; the gloves will prevent the heat transferring from your hands.

To take this to an expert level, the fat can be grated before rubbing in – although I only recommend doing this with butter because of its firmer density. First, freeze your butter block with the wrapper on. When you are ready to make the dough, peel back half of the wrapper, hold the butter block by the still-wrapped half (to stop the heat from your hands transferring to the fat) and grate it straight into your flour using the large teeth of a classic box grater. Once you have grated most of the butter block into the bowl, remove the wrapper and grate the rest.

Try to coat each strand of grated butter in the flour by gently tossing them – this will help to prevent them melting back together. You will now need to use the rubbing-in technique only briefly to achieve the desired texture. Grating the fat into the flour is a lovely way to achieve large, relatively evenly spaced flakes in your crust.

Do not overwork the dough when pie making. In each dough recipe, the instructions I give describe when to stop mixing; this is a crucial moment in the creation of a dough, so pay close attention to it. The moment you see the loose flour gone from the bottom of a mixing bowl it is time to stop! If you continue to mix the dough in a machine or simply knead it for too long, you will overdevelop gluten in the flour. This will result in a dense, elastic dough (think pasta dough) that will be difficult to roll out, shrink away from sides of a tin, lose all flakiness during cooking and generally not be great for pies.

It is important to distinguish the difference in technique between kneading a pie dough and kneading a bread dough. With a pie dough, you are simply bringing the ingredients together into a workable texture, so you no longer see any large clumps of flour or fat. You are handling the dough only lightly, using the most minimal force and stretching possible. With a bread dough, kneading is the opposite. You get your arms going to push, pull and stretch the dough until it is bouncy. The two different techniques achieve the right results for that product.

Rolling out dough

Some people will tell you to only ever roll out dough between two sheets of parchment paper. I find this not to be a great method for a fat-heavy dough (which most of mine are) as the dough always sticks to the paper no matter the temperature. By the time I have managed to roll out the dough thin enough, the fat has melted. I am much more old school. I prefer to dust my work bench and dough with a little flour instead. The key here is not to use too much flour – it is just a light dusting. If you add handfuls of flour to the dough at the rolling-out stage, it changes the ratios and therefore the recipe of the dough itself. Go sparingly and only add more flour when absolutely necessary. Rather than trying to sprinkle flour directly onto the work surface (which will always clump), take a pinch of flour and then, from a height, flick your wrist to let the flour out in a fine cloud above the work bench – pretend you are one of those chefs on a TV cooking show.

Before you start rolling, make sure you have a baking tray lined with parchment paper ready to go. When the dough is rolled thin enough, you can slide the rolled-out dough onto the tray and transfer it straight to the fridge. Remember: prior preparation prevents faffing at crucial moments!

Once your work surface is lightly dusted and your tray is lined with paper, you can start to roll out your dough. At this point, your dough should have been out of the fridge for at least 5 minutes to take the hard chill off it. If your kitchen is very cold and the dough still feels stiff, you can give it a few hard whacks with a rolling pin. In a professional kitchen, this is called 'shocking' the dough.

When the dough feels supple enough to roll out, sit it on the flour-dusted surface and dust a little more flour over the dough. Always start to roll a few centimetres up from the bottom edge of the dough that is closest to you and roll away from you, applying an even pressure as you move away from your body. At the last minute, stop rolling before you reach the top and do not go all the way over the edge. By not rolling all the way over the top and bottom edges, you get a more controlled roll. Rotate the dough 90 degrees and repeat this process. As you repeat the process (always turning

90 degrees in the same direction), check the dough is not sticking to the surface below and dust with a little more flour whenever necessary to prevent that. Once the dough has been rolled out to the required thickness you can even out the slightly thicker edges with the rolling pin to finish. To transfer the rolled-out dough to the lined tray, I find the easiest way is to slide it onto the tray, or roll the dough up around the rolling pin and then unravel it onto the tray. Simply pop the tray into the fridge to chill the dough for the time specified in the recipe.

Lining tins

When it comes to lining a tin, make sure you have as many steps as possible completed ahead of time so that when the crucial moment of putting the dough into the tin comes, everything goes to plan. Fiddling around at the last minute means the dough will get warm, stretch, tear and generally be no fun at all to work with. So, make sure your dough is already rolled out, has been rested and chilled for long enough in the fridge before you attempt to work with it. Make sure that the inside of your tin or mould is greased and/or lined before you take the dough from the fridge. Do not rush this.

If you feel your hands are always very hot, pop on a pair of latex gloves; this will help to stop the heat from your hands transferring to the dough.

When lining a round tin or ring, I drop the disc of dough straight down over the top, making sure it is centred, and then gently lower it down into the base. I then slowly work the dough into the bottom edge around the base, not pushing it too hard against the sides at the beginning and making sure the dough is always centred. Do not stretch the dough or create any folds or overlaps – this may lead to the pie case being thicker in one part and thinner in another place – so take your time to make sure the dough goes down evenly. Once you are happy with how it looks and are sure there are no air bubbles, you can press the dough more firmly into the base and sides of the tin, making sure it goes right down into that bottom edge for a crisp, sharp finish to the crust after cooking.

For any filling that is on the slightly less saucy side (for example, the Butter Pie on page 52), there is a technique known as 'docking' that keeps the pastry base of the pie flat and helps to achieve a crispy bottom. After you have lined the tin or mould but before you add the filling, simply take a fork and prick the base all over. This slows any lamination happening in the base by making sure the fats melt evenly, rather than in pockets, and therefore the base does not rise in flakes. You should not need to do this for a saucy, heavy or dense filling as that will be enough to stop the pastry base from rising. Do not worry about the fork making holes in the pie base, as the moment that the dough softens in the oven, any gaps will close up.

When lining a square or rectangular tin or ring, it is necessary to trim off the corners of the dough to avoid creating some form of overlap or fold in the corners. By trimming off each corner, the pastry will slide easily into the right-angled corners and line the tin or ring perfectly. To achieve this, sit the tin or ring on top of the dough and make two cuts (one vertical and one horizontal) out from the corners to the edge. Remove that square of dough (but keep hold of it as you can use these squares later for decoration). Now, when you drop that dough into the tin or ring, the cut edges will come neatly together. You can gently press the edges into each other where they very slightly overlap.

Adding steam holes and pie chimneys

All pies give off a certain amount of steam as the moisture in both the filling and the dough boil during cooking. Some pies will also release an amount of cooking juices when in the oven. We can limit the amount of cooking juices that come out of a raw pie filling by controlling the internal temperature (one of the reasons it is so important to have a probe thermometer), but it is difficult to prevent all the juices from coming out. When that juice does appear inside a pie, it wants to go somewhere. If it is a large pie and there is no steam hole, the cooking juices will seep out from the weakest point, which is generally why splits occur in a pie crust.

By creating a steam hole, the steam and cooking juices have somewhere to go. Sometimes during the cook those juices will overflow from the steam hole and caramelise on the outside of the crust, like with a Scotch Pie (see page 192). This is known as 'boil out' in the pie world and can look delicious. There are other times, however, when we do not want those juices to spill over and ruin the surface of the pie, for example when making a showstopping piece like the Yorkshire Christmas Pie (see page 98). So, how do we stop that? With a chimney. As outlined in the Pork Pie recipe in this book (see page 122), the steam from the dough and the moisture from the filling can leave the pie via a chimney, allowing the dough to cook properly, stopping the crust from expanding and cracking, but also giving the excess roasted juices an escape route. These juices travel up the chimney, but then as they cool, they drop back down into the pie, keeping in all that important moisture and flavour.

Use the same small cutter to make the steam hole and chimney. Roll some foil around the cutter to make a tube but then roll it a little tighter so it fits snugly into the steam hole. Make sure the foil chimney does not go so far into the pie that it is in contact with the filling or the chimney will not work. Once in place, allow the chimney to unravel slightly so that it is flush against the sides of the steam hole. Always brush a tiny amount of egg wash around where the foil chimney meets the steam hole, to create a seal. The egg wash will seal the chimney the moment it goes in the oven and allow it to do its job properly. I like to make a small collar of dough for a steam hole, which makes it easier to get a tight seal. Take your time when making steam holes and adding chimneys, making sure they are done properly when instructed in the recipes. They will give you a far better finished dish, so it is well worth the effort.

Adding decoration

When adding decoration to a pie, it is important to consider the thickness of the dough you are using for that decoration. You do not want it to be thicker than the main crust itself as it may look a little clumsy after cooking. You can either roll out the dough a touch thinner before cutting out your shapes (bearing in mind they have a tendency to shrink very slightly and therefore get a bit thicker) or you can cut the shapes and then gently thin the dough out with a few pinches (as I do when making pastry leaves, for example) before adding them to the surface of the pie.

Always make sure that the surface of your pie is brushed with egg wash before adding any decoration. Do NOT egg wash the bottom of your decoration or the two surfaces will not stick together. Once the decoration is in place on the pie, return it to the fridge to chill. When I am ready to egg wash the pie again, once the decoration is on and chilled, I make sure that the egg wash goes onto the sides of the decoration where it meets the surface of the pie; this will stop it lifting off during cooking. Never over-egg wash the decoration; just like the rest of the pie, it should be a thin, even coating.

Any scoring should be the very last thing done to the pie before cooking. Do not allow the egg-washed surface of the pie that is to be scored to dry out completely, however, as it will not open nicely during cooking. Instead, the egg wash should only dry enough to feel tacky to the touch. Never egg wash over any scoring (hence why you always do it last) as you will lose the detail and, again, the pastry will not open nicely to reveal that two-tone effect we are after. You do not need to score very deeply to achieve the required effect; I often describe the scoring process

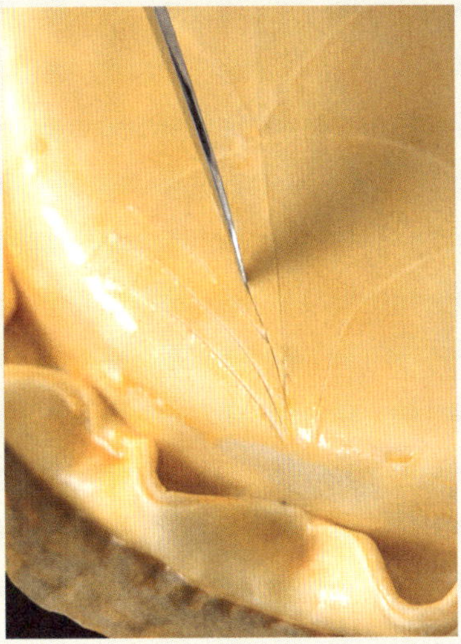

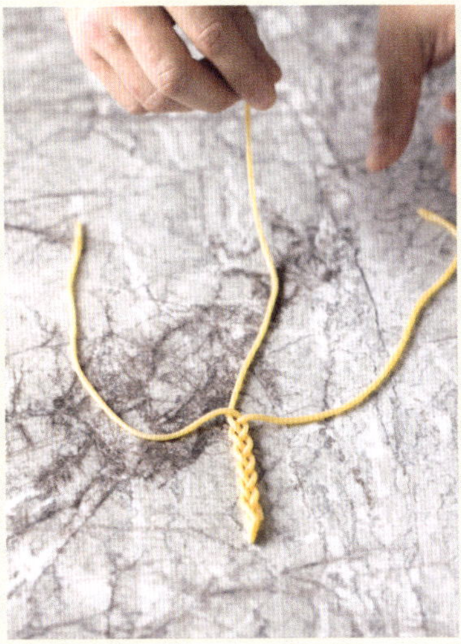

as 'scratching' the surface. Using the tip of a knife that is very sharp always helps.

For lattice work, I recommend using a lattice roller when starting out. You can always progress to cutting a lattice by hand when you feel confident. I use a lattice roller more as a guide, rather than as a cutter, as it never makes all the tiny cuts perfectly. I start rolling the lattice cutter away from me just a few centimetres from the bottom and finish a few centimetres from the top. This will help you lift the roller away from the dough without stretching or tearing the lattice. You can then trim across the top and bottom after with a knife to remove the remaining uncut border. Generally, you will have to go back over all the cut lines with a small knife afterwards to make sure the lattice will open nicely. When doing this, make sure your dough is very cold (your freezer is your friend here).

Try not to handle the lattice too much while cutting it (do not rest your hand on it) as this will soften it quickly. At this point, I gently open up the lattice just a little to make sure it is neatly and evenly cut and I am confident that it will stretch nicely over my surface on application, but do not open up the lattice fully as this makes it much trickier to move and handle. Always pop the lattice back in the fridge for 5 minutes before you apply it to the surface of a pie or over the filling; this will buy you a little more time when attempting to stretch the lattice evenly and position it, making it more of a stress-free experience. Once you have positioned and opened your lattice, gently press down the immediate edges and trim off any excess with a pair of scissors before locking the lattice in place with a crimp.

For the first time, I have used a patterned roller in this book. They can be an uncomplicated way to add instant flair to a pie crust. Nowadays, you can find them easily in craft stores or online. (My top tip is to search for patterned clay rollers used in pottery.) Just make sure your dough is not too cold when firmly rolling the patterned roller over the rolled-out dough, otherwise the design may not transfer effectively. Roll the design onto the dough lid when it is on your work bench. Put a light dusting of flour on the surface but not underneath so that the dough stays in place on the work surface while you roll and comes away easily from the patterned roller. Egg wash the decorated pastry lid only when it is in place on the pie. The egg wash will pool in any indents left behind by the roller and cook to a different shade from the rest of the pie, thereby accentuating the design.

To add decorative braids or twists to a pie, first roll out the dough quite thin (about 3mm) and then freeze it. Once frozen, remove the dough from the freezer.

For a braid, cut three very long, thin strips (about 2–3mm wide) from the frozen dough – these strips must be even in thickness, so use a metal straight ruler as a guide. Gently roll these flat strands on your work bench to take off the sharp edges so that they resemble thin ropes. Lay the three ropes side by side and join them at the top by squeezing together firmly. Trying not to overhandle it and working swiftly with quick movements to avoid transferring heat from your hands to the dough, plait the ropes exactly as you would if braiding hair; pass the right rope over the centre rope, pass the left rope over the new centre rope, then continue crossing the outer ropes over the centre, alternating sides. Once finished, chill the braid for at least 5 minutes before applying it to a surface. They look incredible lined around the lid of a pie or the base of a wellington. Remember, you can always join up two or more shorter braids to make one long braid. If working on a really large pie, you can level up from a delicate braid to something chunkier by using nine ropes of dough and holding three together at a time and repeating the same technique. Do not brush the decorative braid with too much egg wash when in place on the pie surface, as you will lose some of that beautiful detail.

For a twist, cut a thicker strip (about 1cm wide) from the frozen dough, trimming the ends so they taper off. Gently press down one end onto your work bench to secure it in place and turn the other end a few times in one direction to make the twist. Lift the strip off the bench and directly onto the egg-washed pie surface, then chill in the fridge. Any twists need to be very cold when brushing them with egg wash otherwise you will squash them out of shape!

Crimping

Essentially, crimping is the simple technique of joining a pie lid to a base. There are a few fundamentals we need to consider, however, as when done right, a crimp can look spectacular and really elevate a pie. Always leave yourself plenty of dough to crimp with (a 3cm border is usually ideal) as it is easier to trim away any excess than crimp a narrow border. When you join the pie lid to the base, make sure that you thin out the two layers of pastry slightly at that point, otherwise the pastry will be double the thickness here than it is anywhere else on the pie. Your crimping can be an expression of your creativity; you may even reach the point where you build a signature crimp. A very simple way to start is to hold your thumb and forefinger about 3cm apart and then gather the dough between them, pinching the border of dough (the crimp) over and onto the top of the pie – this is the style of crimp you often see on a classic pork pie. As the underside of the dough has now been crimped up onto the lid, remember to egg wash the crimp before baking for an even finish to the pie.

Egg washing

Based on my experience of working with pastry over many years, plus lots of conversations with other experts, I have learned that certain egg washes work better for particular dishes. However, my general rules for egg washing are as follows:

- The egg wash should be pure egg yolk (with no white) to avoid a streaky finish. Let down the egg wash with 1 teaspoon of water per 1 egg yolk. To separate the egg yolk from the white, break the egg into a fine-mesh sieve and allow the chalazae (white stringy bits) to drain through to leave just the yolk.

- When cooking pastry for less than 25 minutes, you can add 1 teaspoon of double cream per 1 egg yolk instead of water to enhance the glaze. (If you add cream to the egg wash when the pastry is cooked for more than 25 minutes, it will go too dark.)

- Any pie needs a maximum of two thin coats of egg wash to achieve a beautiful glaze in the oven.

- Never let the egg wash pool in any dips or gaps in the dough (except when using a patterned roller for a deliberate decorative effect).

- After applying a thin coat of egg wash, dry your pastry brush and use it to wipe away any excess.

- Allow the first coat of egg wash to dry to a tacky or sticky stage before applying the second coat. If you allow it to dry out completely, it will crack in the oven.

- Try not to apply the final coat of egg wash too long before the pie goes into the oven. The egg-washed pastry will come out of the oven with a shiny glaze only if it does not go into the oven dry.

Fillings and textures

You have laboured over your pastry work and are now presenting your stunning, burnished pie at the table. Your eager guests are salivating at the sight of that flaky, golden crust, but they are waiting on that one key moment… the cut through. This is why properly thinking through the filling housed within that pastry is critical. After all that work, you do not want them to be even slightly disappointed by this moment. Flavour is obviously king but one aspect many pie makers do not properly consider is texture. If the pie filling has a soft, saucy texture, do not make it too runny; this will see the filling fall away fully from the pastry crust on cutting, leaving an empty shell and a messy plate. I always err on the side of a thick filling that holds its shape, but this does not mean it needs to be dry. You can add a little potato starch slurry to a sauce to give it more body. I like to serve some extra sauce on the side anyhow, because you can never have too much sauce (just ask the French).

If the finished pie is eaten cold, for example a classic chilled Pork Pie, then the filling must not be too dense as it will not be pleasant to cut, eat or digest. You can lighten these fillings by adding dried breadcrumbs to the mix and/or some cured fats, like lardo or pancetta. Also with a cold pie, consider the visuals of a cut through. Aim to cut all the different ingredients in the pie filling to roughly the same size and combine them well; that way, you will get a beautiful mosaic design on slicing that will wow those who witness it.

PIE MAKING EQUIPMENT

Below are the main items of equipment that I think are indispensable for proper pie making in the home kitchen. They will help you achieve pies of a level that, when you take a step back, you will feel very proud of.

Digital weighing scales

When accuracy is called for, digital weighing scales are perfect for measuring out even the smallest amounts. They are also now relatively inexpensive. Liquids, including water and milk, can be weighed in grams on scales rather than measured in millilitres in a jug – there is virtually no difference in weight and volume of liquids. My digital weighing scales are probably my most used tool in the kitchen, next to an…

Electric stand mixer

This is a bit of a luxury, of course, as a good stand mixer is relatively expensive and it replaces a process that can easily be done by hand. When mixing large amounts of dough, however, it does considerably speed things up. Using a stand mixer also removes from the equation the issue of heat transference from warm hands. I use mine for much more than pie making and so, despite the initial outlay, it has more than paid for itself.

Large mixing bowl

In lieu of a stand mixer, a large mixing bowl is essential when rubbing the fat into flour to make a dough. It is also useful when making fillings and combining pie mixes.

Fine-mesh sieve

Necessary for sifting out any lumps in the flour that would later show up as unsightly raw monstrosities in the cooked pastry. To get a controlled sift into your mixing bowl, gently tap the sieve on the side of the rim with one hand while holding the handle with the other.

Rolling pin

Treat yourself to a long, heavy wooden rolling pin. Due to its own weight, it will do most of the work for you without you having to apply too much pressure. The very best are called American pins. A reasonable length is 40cm or over in order to roll out greater widths of pastry and keep your hands well away from the dough.

Scottish scraper or bench scraper

Sometimes called a bench scraper, a Scottish scraper is a flat, rectangular tool that is useful for gathering dough, dividing pastry into portions and cleaning up work surfaces. It helps keep your work space tidy.

Pie tins, dishes and moulds

I just can't stop buying tins, dishes and moulds in different shapes and sizes: round springform tins, rectangular loaf tins, mousse or savarin rings, ornate vintage copper moulds… Before making a pie, I like to lay out a selection of tins to work out what shape is going to work best. I have specified a tin size and shape for each recipe, so check the equipment section in the recipe ahead of time so you can make sure that you have a similar tin.

Zester

You have two options here: you can be odd like me and cut citrus zest by hand (I get a weird satisfaction out of cutting tiny perfect dice of zest) or you can use a Microplane to finely grate zest (which is 100 times better than using a box grater).

Kitchen scissors

A pair of kitchen scissors are handy to have for trimming the excess pastry from the tops of lined tins and dishes. Victorinox make the best ones for pastry work. They have sharp blades and small, thin handles that don't get in the way, plus they are amazing for the price.

Metal ruler

I use a metal ruler all the time in the kitchen when measuring and cutting pastry. It is easy to clean and good to cut against without damaging anything.

Plain and fluted pastry cutters

Buy a set of plain round cutters and a set of fluted round cutters; either metal or plastic, it doesn't really matter. They are essential for cutting out neat discs of dough and for decorating pastry work.

Shaped cutters and stamps

I buy small, shaped cookie cutters, pastry cutters and stamps all year long. I shudder to think how many I have in my collection. The more I gather, however, the greater freedom I have to be creative with my designs.

Turning knife or paring knife

A small, sharp knife allows for greater control when adding fine detail work to pies, such as scoring the surface of a pie with a decorative pattern or marking the veins on leaves cut from dough.

Lattice roller

If you are new to pastry work, a lattice roller is a foolproof way of making lots of small even cuts in dough that, when opened out, will form a pastry lattice. Both metal and plastic lattice rollers can be easily bought online. Some of the metal ones are quite fancy, but to be honest, I have found the plastic ones to be just as effective.

Small palette knife

Useful for lifting small pastry shapes from your work surface onto a pie, avoiding them becoming too soft from being handled.

Pastry brushes

I have a wide range of brushes; I usually buy them from art shops as they tend to be much better quality and hold on to their bristles longer than the ones sold online. Generally, you don't need any brushes wider than 3cm, but a selection of smaller ones is useful for finer details.

Digital probe thermometer

This is a must, especially for raised pies, as it takes the guesswork out of cooking, which is super important when there is meat involved. If you can, always buy one with a cable that you can close the oven door on so you can leave the probe in the pie while it cooks.

Wire cooling rack

The small feet of a wire cooling rack keep the pie tin lifted off the work surface so there is a constant airflow under the base, which makes it an efficient way of cooling pies.

DOUGHS

Shortcrust Pastry

My most favoured dough for pies is shortcrust pastry; it is genuinely hard to beat for its versatility. This version of shortcrust has been honed over the years to be supple and forgiving, leaving a cooked pie with a buttery mouthfeel, a crisp snap in texture and good definition in the design and decoration. If you follow the instructions carefully and pay attention to a few key principles, this recipe will bring you unbridled joy.

Shortcrust pastry is a laminated dough, in the same way that puff pastry is. The key to a good shortcrust is understanding how the lamination process works. What we want in the dough are nuggets of butter that have not been fully mixed into the flour; those buttery nuggets melt during cooking, leaving empty pockets in the dough that fill with steam (generated by the water content of the butter). As the temperature of the dough rises, those steam-filled pockets expand and create flakes in the pastry.

Knowing that this is how a beautifully flaky crust is created, one fatal mistake must be avoided: overworking the dough. Many cookbooks tell you to aim for a crumble-like consistency when rubbing the butter into the flour for a shortcrust dough… that is a total stitch up! If the dough is overworked at this first stage, you will lose the nuggets of butter that create the flakes in the pastry. The bigger the nuggets of butter, the bigger the pockets and the bigger the flakes. Then if the dough is overworked at the next stage, once all the ingredients have been combined, it will become too elastic. The proteins found in flour bind with water in a dough, then as they are worked, they develop a network of strength that increases in elasticity the more it is kneaded. Consider the way that pasta dough becomes intentionally stretchy as you work it – we do not want that in a pie dough. That elasticity is what makes pastry shrink away from the sides of a tin, compromises the definition in any decorative details and removes the flaky consistency that we all love in a good pie crust. So, follow the recipe as it is set out below and never allow the dough to become too warm (as the butter will seep into the dough and become homogeneous), then you too will fall in love with shortcrust, the king of doughs.

Makes about 1kg (**or enough to line two 25cm round pie tins with some left over for decoration**)

10g fine table salt

60ml ice-cold water

550g plain flour

250g butter, chilled and cut into small cubes

2 eggs, beaten

Method

Dissolve the salt in the ice-cold water and keep it in the fridge until needed.

Sift the flour into the bowl of a stand mixer. Add the butter to the flour and beat with a paddle attachment on a medium speed to incorporate the butter into the flour. Continue mixing until the butter is almost incorporated but tiny nuggets of butter are still visible.

Alternatively, if you don't have a stand mixer and are making the pastry by hand, sift the flour into a mixing bowl and add the butter cubes. Using a round-bladed knife, cut the butter into the flour until the pieces are as small as possible. Working quickly, gently rub the butter into the flour until a similar texture is achieved.

Strain the beaten eggs through a fine-mesh sieve, removing and discarding any stringy strands (the chalazae). Combine the egg and chilled salt water.

Pour the egg mixture into the mixer. Turn the speed to slow and allow it to mix just until there is no flour at the bottom of the bowl. The dough should still be fairly rough.

If making the pastry by hand, create a well in the middle of the flour mix and pour in beaten egg. Gently nudge the flour mix into the centre from the outside edges, bringing everything together until the mix has turned into rough dough and all the loose flour is off the bottom of the bowl.

Finish kneading the dough very lightly on your work surface just until it all comes together. It's important not to overwork the dough or handle it too much.

Flatten the dough into a rectangle, wrap it tightly in clingfilm and chill in the fridge for at least 2 hours before using as directed in the recipe.

Any unused dough can be wrapped tightly in clingfilm and stored in the fridge for up to 1 week or frozen for up to 3 months. If freezing, divide the dough into the quantities needed for individual recipes before wrapping and storing in the freezer – it will take less time to thaw and you won't be wasting any dough. To use any dough from the freezer, thaw it in the fridge overnight.

Cheddar Shortcrust Pastry

While researching the history of the apple pie in the UK, I realised that many of the recipes from the 1800s included actual cheese mixed in with the fruit. Obviously, it is not unheard of to pair cheese with fruit, but rather than add it to the pie filling, I thought that an apple pie in particular would eat better with the cheese mixed into the pastry so that the crust provides a savoury balance to the pie filling, rather than melting through the apples. That is how this Cheddar shortcrust pastry came about; happily, it is the perfect dough for an apple pie and one that I will be always using in the future. It can be deployed for other pies too, with equal success. Try it with those recipes in this book that also have a sweet element to them, such as the Bedfordshire Clanger (see page 128) and the Fidgit Pie (see page 136).

Makes about 1kg (or enough to line two 25cm round pie tins)

10g fine table salt

70ml ice-cold water

180g mature Cheddar

500g plain flour

250g butter, chilled and cut into small cubes

2 eggs, beaten

Method

Dissolve the salt in the ice-cold water and keep it in the fridge until needed.

Finely grate the Cheddar using a Microplane, if you have one, otherwise the fine side of a cheese grater works too.

Sift the flour into the bowl of a stand mixer. Fold the grated cheese through the flour to stop the strands from sticking together.

Add the butter to the flour and cheese and beat with a paddle attachment on a medium speed to incorporate the butter into the flour. Continue mixing until the butter is almost incorporated but tiny nuggets of butter are still visible.

Alternatively, if you don't have a stand mixer and are making the pastry by hand, rub the butter into the flour and cheese in a large mixing bowl until a similar texture is achieved.

Strain the beaten eggs through a fine-mesh sieve, removing and discarding any stringy strands (the chalazae). Combine the egg and chilled salt water.

Pour the egg mixture into the mixer. Turn the speed to slow and allow it to mix just until there is no flour at the bottom of the bowl.

If making the pastry by hand, create a well in the middle of the flour mix and pour in beaten egg. Gently nudge the flour mix into the centre from the outside edges, bringing everything together until the mix has turned into rough dough and all the loose flour is off the bottom of the bowl.

Finish kneading the dough very lightly on your work surface just until it all comes together.

Flatten the dough into a rectangle, wrap it tightly in clingfilm and chill in the fridge for at least 2 hours before using as directed in the recipe.

Any unused dough can be wrapped tightly in clingfilm and stored in the fridge for up to 1 week or frozen for up to 3 months. If freezing, divide the dough into the quantities needed for individual recipes before wrapping and storing in the freezer – it will take less time to thaw and you won't be wasting any dough. To use any dough from the freezer, thaw it in the fridge overnight.

Gluten-Free Shortcrust Pastry

I have included this dough recipe for my gluten-free gang. It can be used as direct replacement for any of the recipes that call for shortcrust pastry. However, do bear in mind that if there is already some gluten in the filling (maybe in the form of breadcrumbs or a roux) then it only reduces the gluten content of the pie rather than removes it entirely. I have been told many times that this dough is as close to a classic shortcrust as it gets whilst being gluten free. It was a recipe developed with my friend Mark Drummond, a hugely talented chef who is known in certain mysterious circles as 'the sausage whisperer'.

Makes about 950g (or enough to line two 25cm round pie tins with some left over for decoration)

10g fine table salt

60ml ice-cold water

500g gluten-free plain flour

5g xanthan gum powder

250g butter, chilled and cut into small cubes

2 eggs, beaten

Method

Dissolve the salt in the ice-cold water and keep it in the fridge until needed.

Sift the flour and xanthan gum powder into the bowl of a stand mixer. Add the butter to the flour and beat with a paddle attachment on a medium speed to incorporate the butter into the flour. Continue mixing until the butter is almost incorporated but tiny nuggets of butter are still visible.

Alternatively, if you don't have a stand mixer and are making the pastry by hand, rub the butter into the flour and xanthan gum powder in a large mixing bowl until the butter is incorporated and the mix is almost a fine crumble consistency. If any nuggets of butter are visible, that is fine – these will form flakes in the crust.

Strain the beaten eggs through a fine-mesh sieve, removing and discarding any stringy strands (the chalazae). Combine the egg and chilled salt water.

Pour the egg mixture into the mixer. Turn the speed to slow and continue to mix just until there is no flour at the bottom of the bowl.

If making the pastry by hand, create a well in the middle of the flour mix and pour in the egg mixture. Gently nudge the flour mix into the centre from the outside edges, bringing everything together until the mix has turned into rough dough and all the loose flour is off the bottom of the bowl.

Finish kneading the dough very lightly once or twice on your work surface just until it all comes together – do not over knead.

Flatten the dough into a rectangle, wrap it tightly in clingfilm and chill in the fridge for at least 20 minutes to keep the butter chilled before using as directed in the recipe.

Any unused dough can be wrapped tightly in clingfilm and stored in the fridge for up to 1 week or frozen for up to 3 months. If freezing, divide the dough into the quantities needed for individual recipes before wrapping and storing in the freezer – it will take less time to thaw and you won't be wasting any dough. To use any dough from the freezer, thaw it in the fridge overnight.

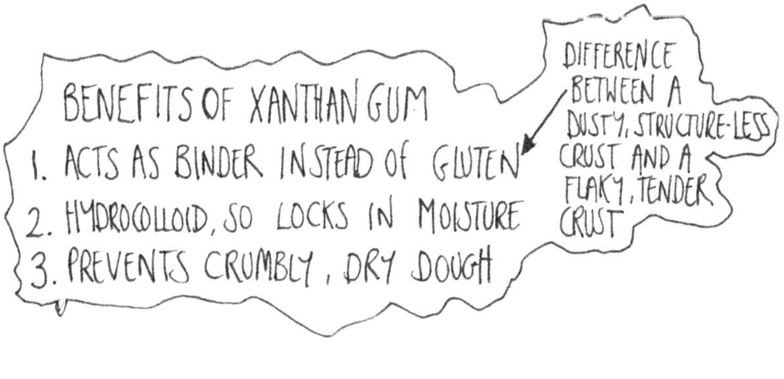

Sweet Shortcrust Pastry

This is a sweet pastry for the ages. The crust has a crumbly but still crisp texture, which provides a wonderful vehicle for any fruit filling. The cornflour does a lot of work behind the scenes here; its starch content helps to set the structure of the pastry and makes the crust a little more tender by reducing the overall protein content of the dough. The ground almonds bring added depth of flavour; however, the inclusion of nuts in the dough means you need to be aware of any allergies when cooking for other people.

Makes about 800g (or enough to line two 20cm pie tins)

340g plain flour

180g butter, chilled and cut into small cubes

170g icing sugar

100g cornflour, sifted

50g ground almonds

2 eggs, beaten

Method

Sift the flour into the bowl of a stand mixer. Add the butter to the flour and beat with a paddle attachment on a medium speed to incorporate the butter into the flour. Continue mixing until the mixture resembles even breadcrumbs. Add the rest of the dry ingredients and combine well.

Alternatively, if you don't have a stand mixer and are making the pastry by hand, rub the butter into the flour in a large mixing bowl until the butter is incorporated and the mixture resembles even breadcrumbs. Add the rest of the dry ingredients and combine well.

Strain the beaten eggs through a fine-mesh sieve into the bowl, removing and discarding any stringy strands (the chalazae).

Turn the mixer speed to slow and allow it to mix just until there is no flour at the bottom of the bowl.

If making the pastry by hand, create a well in the middle of the flour mix and pour in beaten egg. Gently nudge the flour mix into the centre from the outside edges, bringing everything together until the mix has turned into rough dough and all the loose flour is off the bottom of the bowl.

Finish kneading the dough very lightly on your work surface until it all comes together and forms a uniform dough.

Flatten the dough into a rectangle, wrap it tightly in clingfilm and chill in the fridge for at least 3 hours (or overnight) before using as directed in the recipe.

Any unused dough can be wrapped tightly in clingfilm and stored in the fridge for up to 1 week or frozen for up to 3 months. If freezing, divide the dough into the quantities needed for individual recipes before wrapping and storing in the freezer – it will take less time to thaw and you won't be wasting any dough. To use any dough from the freezer, thaw it in the fridge overnight.

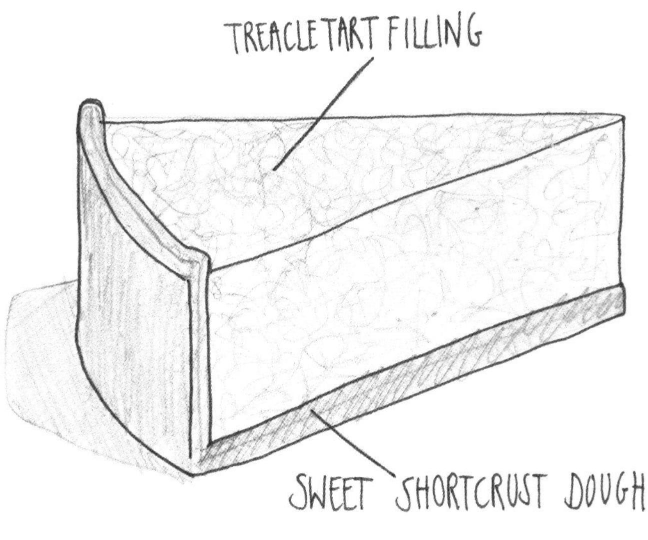

Wholewheat & Rapeseed Oil Pastry

This dough provides a fine crust for the Herb Pie on page 76, but it can also be used for tarts, quiches and all manner of delicious baked goods when cooking vegetarian and vegan dishes. I have specified to use organic, cold-pressed rapeseed oil in the recipe – we have some incredible examples in the UK, such as Duchess Farms or Farrington – but if you struggle to find one you can replace it with a good-quality extra virgin olive oil. Cold-pressed rapeseed oil has the lowest proportion of saturated fats of all vegetable oils and is rich in omega 3 fatty acids. When mixing the dough, do not worry if it looks a little greasy, especially when combining the liquids and flours; the oil will crisp up the pastry beautifully during the cook.

Makes 800g (or enough to line a 23cm tart tin)

5g fine table salt

190g water

130g cold-pressed rapeseed oil

280g wholewheat flour

200g plain flour

Method

Dissolve the salt in the water and then mix with the oil.

Sift both the flours into the bowl of a stand mixer and whisk to combine. Gradually pour the oil mixture into the flour and beat with a paddle attachment on a medium speed to incorporate the oil into the flour. Continue mixing until a rough dough forms and there is no flour left at the bottom of the bowl.

Alternatively, if you don't have a stand mixer and are making the pastry by hand, combine both flours in a large mixing bowl. Create a well in the middle of the flour and gradually pour in the oil mixture, mixing with a wooden spoon to gently nudge the flour into the centre from the outside edges. Continue to bring everything together until a rough dough forms and all the loose flour is off the bottom of the bowl.

Finish kneading the dough very lightly on your work surface just until smooth.

Flatten the dough into a rectangle, wrap it tightly in clingfilm and chill in the fridge for at least 1 hour before using as directed in the recipe.

Any unused dough can be wrapped tightly in clingfilm and stored in the fridge for up to 1 week or frozen for up to 3 months. If freezing, divide the dough into the quantities needed for individual recipes before wrapping and storing in the freezer – it will take less time to thaw and you won't be wasting any dough. To use any dough from the freezer, thaw it in the fridge overnight.

Hot Water Crust Pastry

A rule-breaking dough, hot water crust pastry is revered for its strength that lends structure to bakes. Although once you realise that hot water crust pastry is not in the same family as the laminated doughs (shortcrust, rough puff, full puff), it perhaps is not so rule breaking after all. Rather than flaking, hot water crust pastry just snaps and crumbles during eating. The structure of the dough means it is able to hold up heftier fillings, so it is great for raw meat pies and tall or wide constructions.

The classic hot water crust dough is traditionally made from a rendered animal fat (usually pork lard) heated with water, which is then mixed with flour and a little salt. As it cools, the dough becomes workable enough to mould into a lining for a pie, but once it cools completely, it forms a firm crust. Now, this is brilliant when you have no distractions and quick hands, but it can often turn into a stressful, 'well, I'm never doing that again' experience. To avoid this, the recipe I am offering here includes egg, which keeps the dough a little more supple, and even when fully chilled it remains a joy to work with. The addition of rosemary balances the richness of the lard and gives a wonderful fragrance during baking and eating.

I always encourage making a large batch of hot water crust pastry as it freezes so well. Any trimmings or leftovers can be pressed back into a puck of dough, slightly flattened and then wrapped tightly in clingfilm before chilling (for up to 1 week) or freezing (for up to 3 months; thaw in the fridge overnight).

Makes 1kg

90g water

160g lard

4 rosemary sprigs

8g fine table salt

2 eggs, beaten

550g plain flour

Method

Combine the water, lard, rosemary and salt in a medium saucepan. Gently warm together until the lard has fully melted and everything comes to a simmer. Remove the pan from the heat and set aside to infuse for 5 minutes. Using a fork, remove the rosemary sprigs from the infused lard mixture, then discard the herbs.

Strain the beaten eggs through a fine-mesh sieve, removing and discarding any stringy strands (the chalazae).

Sift the flour into the bowl of a stand mixer fitted with a paddle attachment. Turn on the mixer at a medium speed and pour the lard mixture into the flour, mixing until no more flour is visible at the bottom of the bowl. Finally, pour in the beaten eggs and continue to mix until a smooth dough forms.

Flatten the dough between two sheets of parchment paper and leave to cool to room temperature before chilling for at least 1 hour before using.

Rough Puff Pastry

I would like to think that this recipe is simple enough to convert anyone to puff pastry; the one recipe that finally gives trepidatious bakers the confidence to regularly make puff pastry so good it dazzles all their friends. After all, it is just some flour, butter and a few folds, so there is really nothing to be afraid of! When making a batch of rough puff pastry, I always make more than I need so that there is extra dough to keep for another time; my freezer is constantly crammed with puff. Before rolling out the rough puff dough, weigh and divide it into portions and then freeze it – this is what I call 'virgin dough'. Any trimmings that have been rolled out, formed back into a puck and then frozen will be closer to a good shortcrust pastry, so it will have nice lamination and create flakes but not rise as evenly.

Makes about 1.3kg

10g fine table salt

5g caster sugar

250ml ice-cold water

550g plain flour

500g butter, chilled and cut into small cubes

Method

Dissolve the salt and sugar in the ice-cold water and keep it in the fridge until needed.

Sift the flour into the bowl of a stand mixer. Add the butter to the flour and beat with a paddle attachment on a medium speed for 2–3 minutes to incorporate the butter into the flour. Pour the ice-cold water into the bowl. Continue mixing on medium speed until the dough just comes together – tiny nuggets of butter should be visible throughout the dough.

Alternatively, if you don't have a stand mixer and are making the pastry by hand, rub the butter into the flour in a large mixing bowl until a similar texture is achieved.

Flatten the dough slightly, wrap it tightly in clingfilm and chill in the fridge for 30 minutes.

Take the dough out of the fridge and leave at room temperature for 10 minutes. On a floured surface, roll out the dough to a rectangle measuring 50 × 30cm. Brush off any excess flour from the top surface of the dough and very lightly dampen it with a little water.

With a short side closest to you, visually divide the dough horizontally into thirds. Fold the top third towards you, down over the centre third. Now fold the bottom third away from you, up over the double layer of folded dough. Gently press down on the folded dough and then, using a sharp knife to make 5mm deep cuts, lightly slice along the outer edges of the folds horizontally to release any tension in the dough.

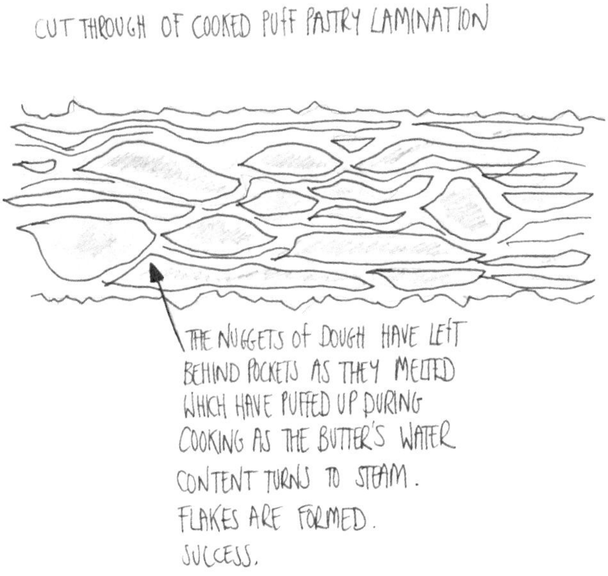

Turn the dough 90 degrees clockwise and repeat the rolling and folding processes. This makes up the first two turns. Tightly wrap the dough in clingfilm and make a mark with an indelible pen in the bottom right-hand corner closest to you. Chill the dough in the fridge for 30 minutes.

Remove the dough from the fridge and leave it at room temperature for 10 minutes. Unwrap the dough and place it on your work surface with the marked corner in its original position. Next, turn the dough 90 degrees clockwise and repeat the rolling and folding processes a further two times to make up the third and fourth turns. Wrap, mark and chill the dough again for 30 minutes.

Again, take the dough out of the fridge and leave at room temperature for 10 minutes. Unwrap the dough, place it on your work surface with the newly marked corner again in the original position. Turn the dough 90 degrees clockwise and repeat the rolling and folding processes two more times to make up the final two turns. (If you are short on time, it is fine to omit the fifth and sixth turns as four turns will still give great lamination.) Wrap and chill the dough for at least 3 hours (or overnight) before using as directed in the recipe.

Any unused 'virgin dough' can be wrapped tightly in clingfilm and stored in the fridge for up to 1 week or frozen for up to 3 months. If freezing, divide the dough into the quantities needed for individual recipes before wrapping and storing in the freezer – it will take less time to thaw and you won't be wasting any dough. To use any dough from the freezer, thaw it in the fridge overnight.

Inverse Puff Pastry

This method of making a puff pastry flips the classic format on its head: rather than the butter being locked inside the dough as you go through the folds, here the butter is always on the outside of the dough. That may sound a little frightening, but bear in mind that the butter is tempered with flour so does not melt on touch. In fact, when making a puff, it is actually more important to understand what is happening with your butter than your dough, so that is what your hands should be feeling. Once you have gotten past the first fold, I think all the subsequent folds in this recipe are actually less stressful than in the classic method because you can feel the suppleness of the butter and whether it is ready to be rolled and folded.

This recipe makes a good amount of puff. Cut however much you need for your recipe straight off the finished dough and then freeze the rest. Given the time invested in making the dough, I think it is sensible to have plenty left over to freeze for use in future recipes.

Makes 1.5kg

For the butter block

500g butter, chilled and cut into small cubes

200g plain flour

For the dough

480g plain flour

150g butter, chilled and cut into small cubes

20g caster sugar

15g fine table salt

190g cold water

5g white wine vinegar

Method

To make the butter block for the outside, first place the diced butter cubes between two sheets of parchment paper and give them a good couple of whacks with a rolling pin to soften them slightly; it is a good way to release any built-up frustration! Transfer the butter to the bowl of a stand mixer fitted with the paddle attachment and beat until uniformly softened. Now add the flour and briefly beat until uniformly mixed.

Using a pencil, draw a 30cm square on one side of a folded piece of parchment paper. Flip the paper over and then flatten the butter mixture inside that square. Fold the excess paper back over the butter to cover it, tucking in any edges. Using a rolling pin, gently flatten the butter mixture to make a perfectly even 30cm square. Chill the butter block in the fridge for 30 minutes.

Meanwhile, make the dough that will be wrapped inside the butter block. Sift the flour into the bowl of a stand mixer. Add the butter to the flour and beat with a paddle attachment on a medium speed to incorporate the butter into the flour. Continue mixing until the mixture is a breadcrumb-like texture and the butter is almost incorporated, but some tiny nuggets of butter are still visible.

Dissolve the sugar and salt in the water and vinegar. Quickly pour the liquid into the mixer whilst beating on a low speed to allow a dough to form, stopping as soon as no more flour is visible on the bottom of the bowl.

Lightly knead the dough on your work surface to make sure it is evenly mixed, but do not overwork it.

Flatten the dough into a 20cm square, wrap it in clingfilm and chill in the fridge for 30 minutes.

Take the butter block out of the fridge and allow it to soften very slightly for about 10 minutes (or a little less if it's very warm in the room).

Place the square of dough in the centre of the butter block at an angle so that the corners of the dough are pointing to the centre of the butter block edges. Fold the corners of the butter block in and over the dough until they meet in the centre like an envelope, wrapping up the dough. Make sure there are no air gaps inside and press together the edges of the butter block to enclose the dough.

Liberally dust your work surface with flour and then roll out this butter-wrapped parcel into a 50 × 20cm rectangle. Dust off any excess flour from the surface of the butter block. With a short side closest to you, visually divide the dough horizontally into thirds. Fold the top third towards you, down over the centre third. Now fold the bottom third away from you, up over the double layer. Gently press down on the folded butter and dough and then, using a sharp knife, lightly slice along the outer edges of the folds horizontally to release any tension in the dough.

Turn the dough 90 degrees clockwise and repeat the rolling and folding processes. This makes up the first two turns. Tightly wrap the dough in clingfilm and make a mark with an inedible pen in the bottom right-hand corner closest to you. Chill the dough in the fridge for 1 hour.

Take the dough out of the fridge and leave at room temperature for 10 minutes to let the butter soften slightly. Unwrap the dough and place it on your work surface with the marked corner in its original position. Next, turn the dough 90 degrees clockwise and repeat the rolling and folding processes a further two times to make up the next two turns. Wrap, mark and chill the dough again for 1 hour.

Again, take the dough out of the fridge and leave at room temperature for 10 minutes. Unwrap the dough, place it on your work surface with the newly marked corner in the original position. Turn the dough 90 degrees clockwise and repeat the rolling and folding processes two more times to make up the final two turns, so six turns have been made in total. Wrap and chill the dough for at least 3 hours (or overnight) before using as directed in the recipe.

Any unused 'virgin dough' can be wrapped tightly in clingfilm and stored in the fridge for up to 1 week or frozen for up to 3 months. If freezing, divide the dough into the quantities needed for individual recipes before wrapping and storing in the freezer – it will take less time to thaw and you won't be wasting any dough. To use any dough from the freezer, thaw it in the fridge overnight.

Beef Dripping Pastry

This pastry is best made with aged beef tallow, which can be ordered online or sourced through your local butcher. The flavour of the beef tallow adds another dimension to a pie crust and it smells amazing while baking; imagine a dry-aged steak searing in a pan. If you can't find aged beef tallow, use the best organic tallow you can source or even some classic beef dripping, if tallow is unavailable.

Makes 800g (or enough to make 4 Scotch Pies)

140g water

160g aged or organic beef tallow (or beef dripping)

6 thyme sprigs

10g fine table salt

500g plain flour

¼ whole nutmeg

1 egg, beaten

Method

Combine the water, beef tallow, thyme and salt in a medium saucepan. Gently warm until everything comes to a simmer. Remove the pan from the heat and leave to infuse for a few minutes. Strain the infused liquid through a sieve, removing and discarding the thyme sprigs.

Sift the flour into the bowl of a stand mixer fitted with a paddle attachment and finely grate in the nutmeg. Turn on the mixer at a medium speed and pour the liquid into the flour, mix until a dough forms.

Strain the beaten egg through a fine-mesh sieve, removing and discarding any stringy strands (the chalazae). Finally, knead the beaten egg into the dough.

Flatten the dough into a rectangle, then wrap it in parchment paper and leave to cool to room temperature before chilling in the fridge for at least 3 hours before using as directed in the recipe.

Any unused dough can be re-formed into a ball, slightly flattened and then wrapped tightly in clingfilm and stored in the fridge for up to 1 week or frozen for up to 3 months. If freezing, divide the dough into the quantities needed for individual recipes before wrapping and storing in the freezer – it will take less time to thaw and you won't be wasting any dough. To use any dough from the freezer, thaw it in the fridge overnight.

Suet Pastry

Suet is specifically the firm, white fat that encases an animal's kidneys. For years, it has been used in shredded form as a fat within British puddings, pies and pastries as its high melting point is useful for keeping dough moist. It adds an almost sponge-like texture to steamed puddings. You can find a shredded version of suet in most supermarkets in the UK, but some online butchers also offer beautiful organic suets. In pudding recipes, I recommend using a vegetarian 'suet' to avoid giving a beefy flavour to your pud!

The use of self-raising flour here means that this dough is best prepared fresh. The raising agents in the flour get to work as soon as they are activated by the liquids, which means it is not suitable for freezing. However, suet pastry is an easy dough to make, so try to make just enough for the recipe and really enjoy the benefits of that sponge-like texture as it cooks. Some of the recipes in this book that use suet do not need the full amount of dough listed here, in which case just halve the quantities given below for those.

Makes about 1kg

10g fine table salt
275ml ice-cold water
550g self-raising flour
120g butter, frozen
210g shredded organic beef suet, very cold
½ teaspoon freshly grated nutmeg

Method

Dissolve the salt in the ice-cold water and keep it in the fridge until needed.

Sift the flour into the bowl of a stand mixer. Grate the frozen butter into the bowl and fold it through the flour, mixing with the paddle attachment on a medium speed until the butter is almost incorporated but tiny nuggets of butter are still visible. Add the suet and nutmeg, then mix briefly until just combined.

Pour the ice-cold salt water into the mixer. Turn the speed to slow and continue to mix just until there is no flour at the bottom of the bowl.

Finish kneading the dough very lightly once or twice on your work surface just until the flour is incorporated but the fat is still visible – do not over knead.

Flatten the dough slightly and wrap it tightly in clingfilm. Put the dough in the fridge and leave to rest for 20 minutes before using.

For a good rise, it is best to use the dough within the next few hours.

SAVOURY PIES

Butter Pie

A pie that is deeply influenced by both religion and immigration, the roots of the Butter Pie are in Lancashire or, more specifically, in Preston. During the mid-nineteenth century, the Irish potato famine caused a growth in immigration to the Preston area, which sits just across the Irish Sea to the east of Dublin. The area already had a substantial Catholic community, which was bolstered further by migrants escaping the famine. In fact, according to the census of 1851, ten percent of Lancashire's population was Irish. Born out of a continued desire to eat pies on a Friday, married with the Catholic practice of avoiding meat on the same day, the Butter Pie became a Friday tradition. Butter Pies are still served up by chippies across the Lancashire region.

The earliest recipes document a pie filling of literally just potatoes cooked in plenty of butter encased in pastry; over time, this evolved into the addition of onion. My version of this classic pie includes a few herbs, along with some garlic, to add subtle layers of flavour. I haven't strayed too far from what a Butter Pie fundamentally is, however, because there is such beauty to its simplicity.

Serves 4–6

800g shortcrust pastry (see page 32 or shop-bought) or you can use Cheddar shortcrust pastry or gluten-free shortcrust pastry (see pages 34–37)

10g softened butter, for greasing

1 egg yolk, strained and beaten with 1 teaspoon water, for egg washing

For the filling

1kg Maris Piper potatoes, peeled

6 rosemary sprigs, 3 left whole and 3 needles picked and finely chopped

25ml vegetable oil

Ingredients & method cont. overleaf

Method

Cut the potatoes lengthways into 1cm thick slices. (For nice big slices, cutting the potatoes lengthways is best.) Rinse the potato slices under cold running water for a minute, then place in a medium saucepan. Add enough water to the pan to cover the potatoes, then add a few good pinches of salt. Bring the water up to a simmer. Taste the cooking water; it should be as salty as sea water and so, if necessary, add more salt to achieve this. Add the 3 whole rosemary sprigs to the water. Cook the potatoes until they are just soft all the way through but not falling apart – this should take around 12–15 minutes. Immediately drain the potatoes, remove and discard the rosemary, and set aside until needed.

Meanwhile, heat the vegetable oil in a wide, heavy-based pan over a medium heat. Add the sliced onion to the pan along with the garlic and 1 teaspoon of salt. Stirring frequently, cook the onions for 20 minutes until nicely caramelised and well browned throughout. If the onions start to catch on the bottom of the pan, add a splash of water to release them. Add 120g of the butter to the pan and allow it to melt into the caramelised onions. Turn off the heat.

In a separate small pan, melt the remaining butter and cook over a medium heat until it caramelises – it will look brown and smell nutty. Pour the browned butter over the caramelised onions and stir well.

Stir 100ml water into the onions, then add the cooked potato slices, spring onions, chopped thyme and chopped rosemary. Season with plenty of freshly ground black pepper. Combine everything well without breaking up the potatoes.

4 large Spanish onions, peeled and thinly sliced

3 garlic cloves, peeled and finely chopped

240g butter

1 bunch spring onions, trimmed and thinly sliced

½ bunch thyme sprigs, leaves picked

Fine table salt and freshly ground black pepper

To serve

Green Herb Sauce (see page 248)

Equipment

20cm mousse ring, 6cm deep (or you can use the ring of a springform cake tin)

Taste a spoon of the filling mixture; if it needs a little more salt, season it now. Set aside to cool to room temperature.

Divide the dough into two pieces, one weighing 500g and the other 300g. On a lightly floured surface, roll out the larger piece to a circle 5mm thick and the remaining dough to a smaller circle 5mm thick. Slide the rolled-out dough onto a baking tray lined with parchment paper and chill in the fridge for 30 minutes.

Grease the inside of the mousse ring with the butter and sit on a baking tray lined with parchment paper. Drape the larger disc of rolled-out pastry over the ring to create the pie base and line the sides of the ring. Press the dough firmly onto the sides of the ring and the baking tray while avoiding any creases, folds or air pockets (see page 18). Trim any excess dough overhanging the top edge of the ring back to 2cm, making a neat collar all the way round. If the dough has become a little soft, place the pastry-lined ring in the fridge for 10 minutes.

Once the pastry is chilled and the filling is at room temperature, fill the pastry case with the potato mixture, making sure that the potato slices sit flat and fill the pastry case without any gaps.

Cut the smaller disc of rolled-out pastry into a 20cm circle, or the same size as the mousse ring, and lay the pastry disc over the potato filling. Brush the outer 2cm of that pastry disc with water, then fold the 2cm collar of overhanging pastry up and over onto the wet border. Gently press down to seal in the filling. This does not need to be especially neat as it will be the base of the pie and not visible.

Line a baking tray with parchment paper and place it on top of the pie, paper side down. Holding the tray firmly in place, flip the whole pie so the top of the pie is now facing upwards – it should be a completely smooth surface. Lightly brush the pastry top with a thin coating of egg wash and refrigerate for 20 minutes.

Preheat the oven to 200°C fan/220°C/gas mark 7.

Remove the pie from the fridge and apply one more thin coating of egg wash. Using the tip of a sharp knife, score your chosen design into the pastry top, making sure not to cut all the way through the pastry layer. I decorated my pie with a simple floral design of nine large petals, scored with diagonal lines inside each petal. Make a small hole in the centre of the pie top which will act as an air vent and and prevent the pastry from cracking.

Place the tray in the centre of the oven and bake the pie for 15 minutes. Lower the oven temperature to 190°C fan/210°C/gas mark 6½ and bake for a further 30 minutes or until the temperature of the filling is above 63°C when tested with a digital probe thermometer. Remove from the oven and allow the pie to rest for 10 minutes. When ready to serve, carefully transfer the pie to a flat plate and remove the ring. If the pie is sticking, slide a small knife around the inside of the ring. Cut the pie into thick wedges and serve with some green herb sauce.

Homity Pie

The Homity Pie could often be found in the restaurants and cafes of 1960s Britain, as the pie gained status as the popularity of vegetarianism grew alongside the hippy movement. An open-top pie usually filled with potatoes, onions, leeks and cheese, the Homity Pie may have originated earlier than the 1960s. It could be as early as 1939, devised in Devon by the Land Girls, who farmed the area during the Second World War, as part of the wartime efforts on the Home Front.

I have added some spinach, mustard and a little lemon zest to cut through the richness of the cream and cheese and make the pie more interesting to eat. And instead of being an open pie, my version of this pie has a top as I think it keeps some of the moisture inside the filling, and that extra crust makes for better balance within the dish.

Serves 3–4

600g shortcrust pastry (see page 32 or shop-bought) or you can use Cheddar shortcrust pastry or gluten-free shortcrust pastry (see pages 34–37)

5g softened butter, for greasing

1 egg yolk, strained and beaten with 1 teaspoon water, for egg washing

For the filling

150g Maris Piper potatoes, peeled and cut into 2cm cubes

50g butter

2 garlic cloves, peeled and finely chopped

1 leek, trimmed of the top 3–4cm of green, washed and thinly sliced

Ingredients & method cont. overleaf

Method

Put the diced potatoes in a large saucepan and pour over enough water to cover them, then add 1 teaspoon of salt. Bring to a simmer over a medium heat and cook the potatoes until a toothpick or small knife goes into the centre without any resistance, but making sure not to overcook them. Drain the potatoes and set aside to cool.

In a medium saucepan, melt 20g of the butter over a low heat. Add the garlic and cook for a few minutes until just softened, then add the leek and cook for a further minute. Finally, add the spinach and cook until just wilted, then season with a pinch of salt and lots of freshly ground black pepper. Tip the contents of the pan into a colander and allow the water drip through, gently pressing the spinach with the back of a large spoon until fairly dry. Add the drained spinach mixture to the blanched potatoes.

Wipe out the pan, then add the remaining butter and melt over a low heat. Stir in the plain flour and gently cook for 3–4 minutes, but without browning. Meanwhile, warm the milk and cream together in a microwave with 1 teaspoon of salt to room temperature. Gradually add the milk mixture to the pan, a ladleful at a time, whisking it in until all the liquid is incorporated to make a smooth roux. Remove the pan from the heat and add the chopped thyme and rosemary, lemon zest, and both mustards, then grate in the cheese and the nutmeg. Fold the vegetables into the sauce and set aside.

Line a baking tray with parchment paper.

250g baby spinach, washed

40g plain flour

150ml whole milk

100ml double cream

1 teaspoon chopped thyme leaves

2 rosemary sprigs, needles picked and finely chopped

Zest of 1 unwaxed lemon

1 heaped teaspoon wholegrain mustard

1 teaspoon English mustard

50g mature Cheddar

¼ whole nutmeg

Fine table salt and freshly ground black pepper

To serve

Dill and Turmeric Pickled Eggs (see page 252)

Equipment

16cm fluted brioche tin, 6cm deep

Divide the dough into two pieces, one weighing 400g and the other 200g. On a lightly floured surface, roll out the larger piece to a 18cm circle, 5mm thick. Roll out the remaining dough to a smaller circle, also 5mm thick. Slide the rolled-out dough onto the lined tray and chill in the fridge for 30 minutes.

Grease the insides of the brioche tin with the softened butter. Check the dimensions of the rolled-out pastry; if it has shrunk a little, roll it back out to an 18cm circle and then drop the pastry disc into the tin. First, press the dough into the base of the tin, then work upwards into the ridges and grooves of the fluted sides all the way to the top edge. Place the pastry-lined tin in the fridge to chill for 20 minutes. Reserve any pastry trimmings to use for decoration later on, so transfer those to the lined tray and rest in the fridge too.

Once the pastry is chilled and the filling is at room temperature, gently press the pastry against the ridges and grooves again, making sure it is in full contact with the tin. Prick the base of the pastry case all over with a fork. Fill the pastry case with the filling mixture; it should come almost to the top but not right to the lip of the tin.

Lay the smaller disc of rolled-out pastry disc over the filling so that it sits neatly on top. Gently press the edges of the pastry lid onto the sides of the tin to seal in the filling. Using a sharp knife, trim away any excess pastry overhanging the top edge of the tin.

Lightly brush the surface of the pastry with a thin coating of egg wash. Using the reserved pastry trimmings, add any decoration you like. I cut three feather shapes and arranged them around the top of the pie. Using a very small pastry cutter or tip of a sharp knife, make a tiny hole or cross in the centre of the pie top which will act as an air vent and allow the steam to escape and prevent the pastry from cracking. Brush the pastry with another thin coating of egg wash. Chill the pie in the fridge for a final 20 minutes.

Preheat the oven to 200°C fan/220°C/gas mark 7.

Remove the pie from the fridge and apply another thin coating of egg wash. Place the tin in the centre of the preheated oven and bake the pie for 30–35 minutes. Remove from the oven and allow the pie to rest in the tin for 10 minutes.

To remove the pie from the tin, place a clean cloth over the top of the pie and pick up the tin with another cloth. Being very careful not to smash the pastry case, quickly flip over the pie, remove the tin, then flip the pie back over and onto a serving plate.

Serve the pie with some of my dill and turmeric pickled eggs and a green salad.

THE

version

I am sharing here

TOOK A FAIR

FEW TRIALS

and a lot of

unlearning

Macaroni Pies

Unless you are a native of Scotland, the fact that the Macaroni Pie is considered almost a national dish there may seem odd to some. Perhaps what people do not realise is how many Italians migrated to Scotland in the late nineteenth century to escape poverty and famine in their home country due to a lack of industrialisation, which led them to seek opportunities elsewhere. These opportunities were often food-related in the form of an ice-cream parlour, a fish and chip shop or a cafe serving up dishes like macaroni, which quickly became a popular ingredient. Originally imported directly from Italy, as demand grew, macaroni was manufactured in Scotland by companies such as Marshalls, who still produce macaroni today, almost a century later. By 1920, Hays bakers of Dundee were advertising the first Macaroni Pies that directly resemble the one we know today; a filling of soft pasta enrobed in a cheese sauce and baked inside a hot water crust pastry shell without a lid.

The version I am sharing here took a fair few trials and a lot of unlearning! During recipe testing, I found that the pasta-to-sauce ratio was invariably wrong; this was a source of confusion because even though I added more sauce each time, I could not get it quite right. Eventually I realised that it was all down to the cooking of the pasta. You do not cook the pasta al dente. For this pie to work, you must cook the pasta a little further than normal – until it is soft all the way through – or it will simply soak up any moisture in the sauce as it cooks inside the pastry.

A sharp Scottish Cheddar is a delight in the mix here, otherwise it is all richness and not enough acidity. The Macaroni Pie does well with that bit of tang. My recipe has the addition of garlic breadcrumbs, which bake on top to give an extra layer of crunchy texture and a further depth of flavour.

Serves 4

- 500g hot water crust pastry (see page 43)
- 15g softened butter, for greasing

For the filling

- 130g elbow macaroni or any other small tube pasta shape
- 50g butter
- 40g plain flour
- 400ml whole milk, warmed

Ingredients & method cont. overleaf

Method

First, cook the pasta. Bring a medium saucepan of water to the boil, add 1 teaspoon of salt and the macaroni, then cook until the pasta is soft all the way through. Drain the macaroni in a colander and then run it under cold water until cooled to room temperature then set aside.

While the pasta is cooking, melt the 50g of butter in a small pan over a medium heat and then add the flour and cook until just starting to brown. Pour in 100ml of the warm milk, whisking until smooth. Whisk in another 100ml of the milk and repeat until all the milk has been added and you have a smooth sauce. Fold in all of the grated Cheddar and 40g of the grated mozzarella. Allow the cheese to sit in the heat of the sauce for a minute, then gently mix until smooth. Stir in 1 teaspoon of salt and a generous amount of freshly ground black pepper. Set aside to cool.

60g mature Cheddar, grated

120g mozzarella, grated

1 teaspoon English mustard

¼ bunch chives, finely chopped

Zest of 1 unwaxed lemon

40g Garlic Breadcrumbs (see page 258)

Fine table salt and freshly ground black pepper

To serve

Steamed green beans

Spiced Tomato Chutney (see page 254)

Equipment

Four 10cm round foil pie dishes or non-stick pie tins (about 4cm deep)

On a lightly floured surface, roll out the pastry to a square about 5mm thick. Press or cut out four 14cm discs.

Lightly grease the insides of the foil dishes or tins with the butter. Line the greased dishes or tins with the pastry discs, making sure that the dough goes right into the edges of each base and avoiding any folds, creases or air pockets. Using a fork, prick the bottoms of the pie cases all over. Do not trim the excess dough from the tops of the dishes or tins to neaten the pies; a rustic look is key here. Place the pastry-lined dishes or tins in the fridge to chill for 15 minutes.

Once the sauce has cooled, stir in the mustard, chives and lemon zest, along with the remaining grated mozzarella. Finally, fold the cooked pasta through the sauce.

Preheat the oven to 200°C fan/220°C/gas mark 7.

Fill each pie case with a quarter of the filling. Cut four small discs of parchment paper and sit them on top of the pies to cover the surface of the filling.

Place the pie dishes or tins on a baking tray in the centre of the preheated oven and bake the pies for 20 minutes. Peel off the paper and scatter the garlic breadcrumbs over the top of the pies. Lower the oven temperature to 185°C fan/205°C/gas mark 4½ and bake for a further 15 minutes.

Serve the pies within 20 minutes of taking them out of the oven so that the cheese oozes and pulls into strings when the pies are cut open. Enjoy with a few steamed green beans and a little spiced tomato chutney on the side.

THE ICONIC NARDINI CAFE IN LARGS, A MONUMENT TO ITALIAN IMMIGRATION IN SCOTLAND

Woolton Pie

Named after Lord Woolton, who became Britain's wartime Minister of Food in 1940, this pie was created in the kitchens of The Savoy hotel. It demonstrated how hearty dishes could be created in times of rationing and hardship during the Second World War. The official recipe (taken from the *Bromley and District Times* in February of 1941) contained potato, swede, carrot and cauliflower with a sauce made of water thickened with oatmeal; it showcased homegrown vegetables from the many allotments that were set up to support the war effort and combat food shortages. I like to imagine that, as the Woolton Pie gained in popularity across the country, people may have incorporated other vegetables into the filling – the odd parsnip, a few leeks, maybe...

The original Woolton Pie had a filling largely made up of basic root vegetables and, when sliced, was probably slightly drab in appearance. This version, with its colourful layers, has a showstopping cut-through at the table. In the spirit of Lord Woolton, I have kept this pie vegetarian while using some other ingredients that are readily available now, although they wouldn't have been during the time of rationing. Dig for victory. And enjoy some lovely pine nuts.

Serves 6

- 800g shortcrust pastry (see page 32, or shop-bought), or gluten-free shortcrust pastry (see page 36)
- 15g softened butter, for greasing
- 1 egg yolk, strained and beaten with 1 teaspoon water, for egg washing

For the filling

- 1 medium butternut squash, peeled, halved, deseeded and cut into 5mm slices
- 50ml extra virgin olive oil
- 2 red onions, peeled and cut in half through the roots
- 2 rosemary sprigs, needles picked and finely chopped

Ingredients & method cont. overleaf

Method

Preheat the oven to 200°C fan/220°C/gas mark 7 and line a roasting tray with foil.

Rub the squash slices with half of the olive oil, then spread them out over the foil-lined tray. Place the tray in the preheated oven and roast the squash for 10 minutes.

Cut each red onion half into 6 wedges and dress with the remaining oil. Add the onions to the tray with the part-roasted squash and sprinkle over the chopped rosemary and a few pinches of salt. Return the tray to the oven and roast the veg for a further 12 minutes. Remove from the oven and set aside to cool.

In a wide-based pan with a lid, bring a few tablespoons of water to a simmer over a medium heat. Add the spinach to the pan, pop on the lid and cook for 2 minutes. Remove the lid, sprinkle in a few pinches of salt, then quickly stir the spinach with a wooden spoon to finish steaming. Drain the spinach in a colander. Using the back of a large spoon, press the spinach against the colander to expel any excess water. Spread the spinach out in the colander to cool slightly.

Wrap the spinach in a clean dish cloth or kitchen towel, then squeeze out any remaining moisture. Transfer the spinach to a chopping board and roughly chop it.

400g spinach

200g feta cheese, crumbled

100g toasted pine nuts

1 jar (350g drained weight) mixed roasted peppers, seeds removed

50g capers, roughly chopped

Fine table salt

Equipment

20cm non-stick springform cake tin

In a large mixing bowl, combine the spinach with the crumbled feta. Fold in the toasted pine nuts and set aside.

Line a large baking tray with parchment paper. Divide the dough into two pieces, one weighing 500g and the other weighing 300g. On a lightly floured surface, roll out the larger piece to a 35cm circle, 5mm thick. Roll out the remaining dough to a 24cm circle, also 5mm thick. Trim away any excess pastry. Slide the rolled-out pastry onto the lined tray and place in the fridge to chill for at least 20 minutes. Reserve any pastry trimmings to use for decoration later on; transfer those to the lined tray and rest in the fridge too.

Grease the insides of the cake tin with the butter. Line the tin with the larger disc of rolled-out dough (see page 18), pressing the dough firmly onto the sides of the tin, but avoiding any creases, folds or air pockets. Using kitchen scissors, trim any excess dough overhanging the top edge of the tin back to 3cm, making a neat collar all the way round. Place the pastry-lined tin in the fridge to chill for 15 minutes.

Take the tin out of the fridge and layer half of the roasted squash mixture into the pastry case, keeping the layer as flat as possible. Cover the bottom layer with half of the roasted peppers, then sprinkle over half of the chopped capers. Top this with all of the spinach, feta and pine nut mixture, spreading it out evenly. Next, add the remaining roasted peppers and capers before topping with the remaining squash mixture, flattening everything down.

Lightly brush the overhanging collar of dough with a little water, then place the smaller disc of dough across the top to make the lid, pinching the two layers together firmly to seal. Lightly brush the pie lid with a thin coating of egg wash. Crimp the sealed edges back onto the lid (see page 25). Add any decoration you like on the top – I added some pleated detail around the edges and then added some twisted pastry strips (see page 23). Chill in the fridge for 15 minutes.

Preheat the oven to 190°C fan/210°C/gas mark 6½.

Lightly brush the pie with a final thin coating of egg wash, this time including the crimp and any decoration. Place the tin in the centre of the preheated oven and bake the pie for 45 minutes.

Remove from the oven and allow the pie to rest for 10 minutes in the tin, before releasing it from the tin. Slide the pie onto a serving plate or stand. Cut nice big wedges of the pie to serve with a light green salad or baby gem leaves dressed with a chive vinaigrette.

Likky Pie

Originating in Cornwall, the Likky Pie is a savoury pie with a filling of leeks cooked in a milk and butter sauce, all topped by a suet crust. Sometimes sharp Cheddar is crumbled between the layers of leeks, and often fat strips of bacon are laced through the filling. For me, the inclusion of salty bacon can hammer the leek flavour into submission and the fat rendered by the bacon can split the sauce, so I have chosen to leave out the bacon altogether, keeping the dish meat-free. Instead, I have focused on driving more flavour into the leeks by roasting them first to intensify their natural sweetness. To complement the leeks without overpowering them, I scatter in a little bit of blue cheese and a few toasted hazelnuts.

Serves 4–5

700g shortcrust pastry (see page 32, or shop-bought), or gluten-free shortcrust pastry (see page 36)

15g softened butter, for greasing

1 egg yolk, strained and beaten with 1 teaspoon water, for egg washing

For the filling

12 medium leeks, washed and outer leaves removed

30ml extra virgin olive oil

4 garlic cloves, peeled and crushed or minced

Handful of thyme sprigs

220g Stilton cheese, crumbled

100g toasted hazelnuts, lightly crushed

Fine table salt and freshly ground black pepper

Photographed overleaf

Method

Preheat the oven to 190°C fan/210°C/gas mark 6½ and line a roasting tray with foil.

Trim the green tops from the leeks so that each leek is slightly longer than your loaf tin – my tin is 21cm, so I trimmed to the leeks to 24cm long. Rub the leeks with olive oil and season with 1 teaspoon of salt. Lay the leeks in the foil-lined tray and scatter over the garlic and thyme sprigs. Cover with foil to seal.

Roast the leeks in the oven for 20 minutes. Remove the top sheet of foil and continue to roast the leeks for 25 minutes. Remove the tray from the oven, discard the garlic and thyme and set the leeks aside to cool.

Meanwhile, line a large baking tray with parchment paper. On a lightly floured surface, roll out two-thirds of the pastry dough to a 40 × 25cm rectangle, 5mm thick. Roll out the remaining dough to a 28 × 18cm rectangle, also 5mm thick. Trim away any excess pastry. Slide the rolled-out pastry onto the lined tray and place in the fridge to chill for at least 30 minutes. Reserve any pastry trimmings to use for decoration later on, so transfer those to the lined tray and rest in the fridge too.

Lightly grease the insides of the loaf tin with the butter. Cut a long, thin strip of parchment paper slightly narrower the width of the tin's base, then lay it inside the tin so that the base and ends are covered and any excess paper hangs well over each end. (The paper will be used to lift the pie out of the tin after baking.)

Remove the large rectangle of rolled-out pastry from the fridge and lay it on a sheet of parchment paper. Sit the loaf tin in the centre of the pastry, aligning the long sides of the tin to the long sides of the pastry.

To serve

Pickled Beetroot, Apple and Mint Salad (see page 262)

Equipment

900g (2lb) non-stick loaf tin

Using a sharp knife, cut a diagonal line from each corner of the tin to the nearest corner of the pastry; these cuts will make it easier to line the tin neatly. Next, carefully lower the pastry sheet into the tin – the diagonal cuts should allow the pastry to fall neatly and evenly to the bottom. Gently press the dough into the sides of the tin, making sure the dough settles right down into the creases and allowing it to form overlaps in the corners where the diagonal cuts were made. Trim away some of the excess pastry from the corners but leave enough to seal the seams when firmly pressed together (see page 20). There should be about 3cm of pastry overhanging the top edge of the tin all the way round – do not trim this collar. Chill in the fridge for at least 20 minutes.

Remove and discard any leaves from the roasted leeks that are burnt – browned is totally fine, blackened is not. Cut each leek in half lengthways. Season the cut sides of the leeks with 1 teaspoon of salt and lots of freshly ground black pepper.

Cover the base of pie case with a layer of leeks with their flat sides facing downwards. Scatter over a little of the crumbled Stilton and crushed hazelnuts. Repeat these layers until all the leeks, Stilton and hazelnuts have been used up.

Lightly brush the collar of pastry overhanging the edges of the tin with a little water. Lay the smaller rectangular pastry lid directly over the top of the pie case. Using your fingers, firmly squeeze together the two layers of pastry where the lid meets the collar to thin the pastry and seal the pie. Neaten this collar of pastry by trimming it back to an equal length all the way round.

Lightly brush the surface of the pastry with a thin coating of the egg wash. Crimp the overhanging collar of pastry up and onto the lid of the pie (see page 25). Using the reserved pastry trimmings, add any decoration you like. I added an Art Nouveau-inspired floral design with tendrils growing out of elongated leaves and with tiny dots for petals. Using a very small pastry cutter or tip of a sharp knife, make a tiny hole in the centre of the pie top which will act as an air vent and prevent the pastry from cracking. As a finishing touch, I cut a thin ring of pastry to add a lip to the steam hole. Brush the pastry with another thin coating of egg wash. Chill the pie in the fridge for 15 minutes. Finally, add another thin coating of egg wash, this time including the crimp.

Preheat the oven to 200°C fan/220°C/gas mark 7.

Place the tin in the centre of the oven and bake the pie for 45 minutes. Remove from the oven and allow the pie to rest in the tin for 10 minutes. Using the strip of parchment paper, gently and carefully lift the pie out of the tin.

This pie can be served either hot or cold, cut into 3cm-thick slices with a serrated bread or pastry knife, and pairs really nicely with the pickled beetroot, mint and apple salad.

Onion Pie

A few years ago, I read Simon Hopkinson's beautiful recipe for My Mother's Lancashire Cheese and Onion Pie in *The Good Cook*, the book that accompanied his TV series of the same name. I loved the simplicity of the ingredients: the acidity of the cheese alongside the sweetness of the onions, and the rooting of the pie in Lancashire. There are eighteenth-century recipes, including one by Hannah Glasse, that are also known as Onion Pie. These often contained a slightly more elaborate list of ingredients, including potatoes, eggs and apples. As mentions of the Onion Pie move into the twentieth century, however, the pie becomes a working-class staple around the North West of England and was simply cheese and onion in a shortcrust dough (sometimes with a little lard in it to cut the amount of butter). I've given the pie a little glow-up with a pleated lattice finish that is simple to do but really quite striking looking when cooked. Using rough puff pastry here instead of shortcrust suits this finish better, as the lamination in the dough helps keep the pleating tight while it puffs up. My recipe here includes a splash of sherry vinegar which acts as a lovely foil to the earthy onions.

Serves 6

- 500g rough puff pastry (see page 44, or shop-bought puff pastry)
- 1 egg yolk, strained and beaten with 1 teaspoon water, for egg washing
- 1 teaspoon onion seeds, for sprinkling

For the filling

- 1 red onion
- 1 brown onion
- 8 round shallots
- 3 banana shallots
- 30ml extra virgin olive oil
- 2 garlic cloves, left whole in their skins

Method

Preheat the oven to 190°C fan/210°C/gas mark 6½ and line a roasting tray with foil.

Peel all the onions and shallots, then cut each one in half through their roots. Set aside the small round shallots and roughly cut all the others into 1cm wedges, again through their roots. Toss them all in the extra virgin olive oil and 1 teaspoon of salt and scatter over the foil-lined tray. Nestle the garlic cloves (in the skins) in there too.

Place the tray in the oven and bake the onions and shallots for 25 minutes or until they are nicely browned. Turn off the oven.

Remove the garlic cloves from the tray and allow them to cool for a few minutes, then squeeze out their soft interior, discarding the skins. Stir the soft garlic into the roasted onions and shallots.

Transfer everything from the tray to a medium saucepan and cook over a gentle heat for 5 minutes to soften the veg a little more, then mix in the thyme and vinegar. Check the seasoning, adding a pinch of salt, if necessary. Set aside to cool. Once the filling mixture reaches room temperature, fold in the grated cheese.

Ingredients & method cont. overleaf

8 thyme sprigs, 6 leaves picked, 2 leaves picked and finely chopped

20ml sherry vinegar

100g Lancashire cheese or tangy mature Cheddar, grated

Fine table salt

Line a baking tray with parchment paper. On a lightly floured surface, roll out the puff pastry to a rectangle about 35 × 23cm and 5mm thick. Slide the rolled-out pastry onto the lined tray and place in the fridge to chill for 20 minutes (or 10 minutes in the freezer).

Preheat the oven to 200°C fan/220°C/gas mark 7.

With it still on the parchment-lined tray, spoon the roasted onion and shallot mixture onto the centre of the pastry strip in a channel down its length, stopping about 2cm from each end. Starting where the filling begins, make a series of diagonal cuts in the pastry away from the filling to the edges of the dough on both sides, leaving about 1.5cm between each cut.

Starting at the end furthest away from you and working towards you, fold one pastry strip made by the diagonal cuts over the filling. (Do not fold over the pastry at the very end before the first cuts; that will be used to seal the filling at the end of the folding process.) Lightly brush the folded pastry strip with a little egg wash, then fold over its counterpart from the opposite side, placing it on top of the first strip. Lightly brush that with egg wash too. Continue this process, folding alternate pastry strips from opposite sides all the way down the length of the filling to form a lattice. Use the two pieces of pastry at the top and bottom ends to seal in the ends of the filling, trimming away any excess pastry, if necessary. Lightly brush the entire pie with a thin coating of egg wash, making sure all the exposed pastry is coated. Sprinkle the onion seeds all over the surface of the pastry lattice.

Place the tray in the centre of the oven and bake the pie for 35 minutes or until the pastry is nicely puffed and has a caramel colour. Remove from the oven and leave the pie to cool for 5 minutes before slicing with a serrated knife. Serve with a green salad for a light lunch.

Herb Pie

There is a recipe for Herb Pie in Elizabeth Raffald's 1769 book, *The Experienced English Housekeeper*. It was created for Lent and as such was devised to use up a multitude of green leafy vegetables, including beet leaves, spring greens, spinach and parsley, that would have been thickened with oats and butter. I love the idea of eighteenth-century cooks making (relatively) healthy and nourishing pies with greens, rather than just the meat-based classics.

In my version of Herb Pie, I have avoided the usual dairy or animal fats in the pastry dough. Instead, I have created a much lighter pie crust using wholewheat flour that relies on rapeseed oil for its structure. If you prefer, you can replace the rapeseed oil directly with olive oil. And feel free to experiment with the herbs that go into the filling; different herbs will alter the flavour profile of the pie depending on how they complement each other. For the cheese, I have used Graceburn, which is similar to feta but made with raw cow's milk. If you cannot source Graceburn, regular feta made with sheep's milk is a good swap.

Serves 4

800g wholewheat & rapeseed oil pastry (see page 42)

15g softened butter, for greasing

1 egg yolk, strained and beaten with 1 teaspoon water, for egg washing

For the filling

750g spinach, washed

20ml vegetable oil

1 brown onion, peeled and thinly sliced

3 eggs, beaten

1 bunch flat-leaf parsley, leaves picked and roughly chopped

1 bunch basil, leaves picked and roughly torn

Method

Line a baking tray with parchment paper. Divide the dough into two pieces, one weighing 500g and the other weighing 300g. On a lightly floured surface, roll out the larger piece to a 45 × 20cm rectangle, about 5mm thick. Roll out the remaining dough to a smaller 40 × 15cm rectangle, also 5mm thick. Slide the rolled-out dough onto the lined tray and chill in the fridge for 30 minutes.

In a wide-based pan with a lid, bring a few tablespoons of water to a simmer over a medium heat. Add the spinach to the pan, pop the lid on and cook for 2 minutes. Take the lid off, sprinkle in a few pinches of salt, then quickly stir the spinach with a wooden spoon to finish steaming. Transfer to a bowl.

In the same pan, warm the oil over a medium heat. Add the onion to the pan and cook for a few minutes until just softened. Add the wilted spinach, then drain in a colander. Using the back of a large spoon, press the spinach against the colander to expel any excess water. Spread the spinach out in the colander to cool slightly.

Wrap the onion and spinach in a clean dish cloth or kitchen towel, then squeeze out any remaining moisture. Transfer the mixture to a chopping board and roughly chop.

Ingredients & method cont. overleaf

½ bunch dill, leaves picked and roughly chopped

½ bunch mint, leaves picked and roughly chopped

100g cooked red beetroot, cut into 1cm cubes and patted dry

250g Graceburn or feta cheese, crumbled

Fine table salt and freshly ground black pepper

To serve

Tomato, Red Onion and Sherry Vinegar Salad (see page 260)

Equipment

36 × 12cm rectangular loose-bottomed tart tin

Textured wooden rolling pin with the design of your choice (optional)

In a large mixing bowl, combine the onion and spinach with the beaten eggs and chopped and torn herbs. Season with 1 teaspoon each of salt and pepper. Finally, fold in the diced beetroot and crumbled Graceburn or feta cheese.

Preheat the oven to 200°C fan/220°C/gas mark 7 and grease the tart tin with the butter.

Line the greased tart tin with the larger rectangle of dough (see page 20). Prick the bottom all over with a fork. Fill the tart case with the filling mixture. If you are using a patterned rolling pin, you can decorate the smaller rectangle of dough for the lid now – I used a wooden rolling pin etched with wavy lines to create a decorative pattern before adding the lid to the pie. Lay the smaller rectangle of dough on the top and seal the edges together. Trim off any excess pastry overhanging the lip of the tin with a sharp knife, then lightly brush the pastry lid with a thin coating of the egg wash. Place the pastry-lined tin in the fridge to chill for 30 minutes.

Lightly brush the pastry lid with a final thin coating of the egg wash. If you are using the tip of a sharp knife to score a decorative design into the top of the lid, you can do that now.

Place the tin in the centre of the oven and bake the pie for 45 minutes, turning the pie 180 degrees in the oven halfway through the cooking time. Remove from the oven and leave the pie to rest in the tin for 30 minutes before lifting it out and slicing.

Serve slices of the pie with the tomato, red onion and sherry vinegar salad.

Lobster Cannelons

One of my favourite discoveries while researching this book, the Lobster Cannelon was something totally new to me when I came across it in Frederick T. Vine's book, *Savoury Pastry*, from 1900. Sold in pie shops and bakeries of the late nineteenth and early twentieth centuries, the technique for making these pastry tubes is brilliant. I found an early reference to them in the *Kendal Mercury*, which reprinted the menu for a Mayor of Kendal's dinner on 14th March 1863, where they sat alongside calves' foot jelly, oyster patties and saddles of mutton. I have a suspicion that the name cannelon was French influenced, probably around the time that the master chefs of Paris, such as Auguste Escoffier, came over to cook in the grand hotels and royal courts of London. The Latin word *canneolus* means a joint of cane; in Roman times, pastry would have been wrapped around canes and cooked. Of course, the link to cannoli, the Italian dessert of fried dough filled with cream, is also obvious.

The key to these Lobster Cannelons is the wooden sticks that you wrap the pastry around; just make sure you soak them in water first so they do not burn in the oven. I found some small wooden rolling pins online that are about 3cm in diameter and 16cm long, the perfect size for making cannelons. Once you have learned the technique, feel free to play around with the fillings; bakery counters would have been full of different flavours in Vine's time.

Serves 4

- 400g inverse puff pastry (see page 46, or shop-bought puff pastry)
- 20g softened butter
- 1 egg yolk, strained and beaten with 1 teaspoon water, for egg washing

For the filling

- 200g crème fraîche
- 100g cooked crayfish tails, shelled and cut in half
- 100g cooked lobster meat, roughly chopped
- 2 celery sticks, peeled and finely chopped

Method

An hour before starting the recipe, place the wooden rolling pins in a bowl of water to soak.

At the same time, sit the crème fraîche on a few layers of kitchen towel on a plate to remove some of the moisture and place in the fridge.

Line a baking tray with parchment paper. On a lightly floured surface, roll out the pastry to a 30 × 20cm rectangle, just under 5mm thick. Slide the rolled-out pastry onto the lined tray and place in the fridge to chill for 25 minutes (or 15 minutes in the freezer).

Meanwhile, remove the rolling pins from the bowl and pat dry to remove any excess water. Cut four rectangles of parchment paper large enough to fit neatly around the rolling pins. Brush the soaked rolling pins with the softened butter and then wrap each one in a piece of paper – if the paper overlaps, use a touch more butter to keep things neat. Brush the paper-wrapped rolling pins all over with more butter.

Ingredients & method cont. overleaf

1 avocado, peeled and roughly chopped, dressed with 1 teaspoon lemon juice

1 Granny Smith apple, peeled, cored and finely chopped

3 tarragon sprigs, leaves picked and roughly chopped

¼ bunch flat-leaf parsley, leaves picked and roughly chopped

Zest of 1 unwaxed lemon

¼ teaspoon Tabasco sauce

Fine table salt

Equipment

Four small wooden rolling pins (about 3cm in diameter)

Take the rolled-out pastry and cut it into four long strips. Lay one strip in front of you at a slight diagonal angle. Place the base of one the rolling pins on the end of the pastry strip furthest away from you and, keeping the pin horizontal, roll the pin towards you – allow the pastry strip to slightly overlap at the edges with each rotation until it reaches the end of the pin. Tuck the loose end of pastry in on itself to form the base of the cannelon. Lay the cannelon still on its rolling pin on the lined tray. Repeat this process with the other three rolling pins and pastry strips. Place the cannelons on the tray in the freezer to chill for 15 minutes.

Preheat the oven to 185°C fan/205°C/gas mark 6½.

Lightly brush the cannelons all over with a thin coating of egg wash. Place the tray in the centre of the preheated oven and bake the cannelons for 25 minutes or until the pastry is fully puffed and a deep caramel colour. Set aside to cool for 10 minutes before removing the rolling pin and paper.

Meanwhile, prepare the filling. Scrape the crème fraîche from the kitchen towel into a small mixing bowl. Add the crayfish, lobster, celery, avocado, apple, herbs, lemon zest, Tabasco sauce and 1 teaspoon of salt, then mix well.

Once the cannelons are cool, using a small spoon, fill the pastry tubes with the lobster mixture, packing it all the way down the tubes.

Serve the cannelons as a light summer snack while pretending you have just walked out of a Victorian pie maker's shop on payday.

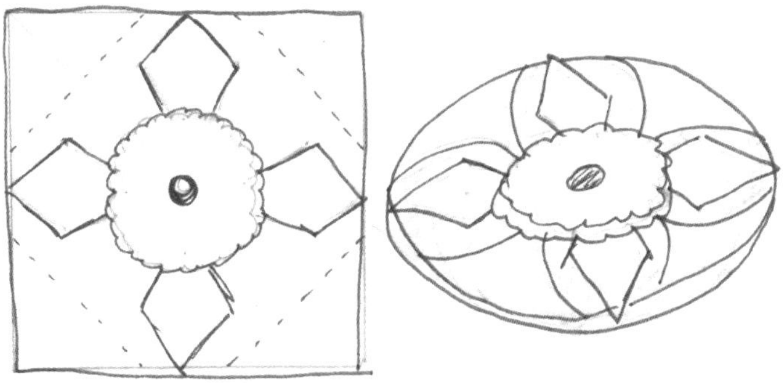

PASTRY DESIGN DETAILS TAKEN FROM FREDERICK T VINE'S "SAVOURY PASTRY" OF 1900

Prawn Patties

I was directed to Frederick T. Vine's 1900 publication, *Savoury Pastry*, by the incredibly knowledgeable food historian, Ivan Day. Vine wrote a extensive collection of works on how to operate a professional bakery; his books offer a snapshot of which dishes were popular in those times. I am privileged to have held an original copy of *Savoury Pastry* in the Rare Books Reading Room of the British Library and had the time to study it properly. In all honestly, I can say that the British population's preferences have not changed all that much in over 100 years.

Much like the Lobster Cannelons on page 80, these patties were sold alongside other savoury pastries in pie shops at the beginning of the twentieth century, and Vine shows how to decorate them. Here, I have stayed true to their original construction (similar to building a vol-au-vent) and have simply updated the filling to reflect modern tastes.

Serves 4

500g inverse puff pastry (see page 46, or shop-bought puff pastry)

1 egg yolk, strained and beaten with 1 teaspoon water, for egg washing

For the filling

80g butter

1 tablespoon vegetable oil

1 brown onion, peeled and finely chopped

1 red chilli, deseeded and finely chopped

1 red pepper, deseeded and cut into 1cm cubes

20g ginger, grated

2 garlic cloves, peeled and finely chopped

Method

Line a baking tray with parchment paper. On a lightly floured surface, roll out the pastry to a large rectangle, around 5mm thick. Slide the rolled-out pastry onto the lined tray and place in the fridge to chill for 30 minutes (or in the freezer for 15 minutes).

Using a 10cm round pastry cutter, press out eight discs from the sheet of pastry. Leave four of those pastry discs whole and set aside. From each of the other four pastry discs, punch out a smaller disc from the centre using an 8cm round cutter. Separate the outer ring of pastry from the inner 8cm discs.

Lightly brush the four 10cm pastry discs with a thin coating of egg wash, then lay the pastry rings on top, aligning the outer edges. Pop all the pastry back into the fridge to chill for 15 minutes (or in the freezer for 5 minutes).

Preheat the oven to 200°C fan/220°C/gas mark 7.

Take the 10cm pastry discs with the outer rings in position and, using a fork, prick all over the centre base but do not prick the ring. (Pricking the base stops it rising in the centre and allows the un-pricked sides to rise, giving the pastry case its shape.) Lightly brush the top of the ring only with a thin coating of egg wash. (Be careful not to get egg wash on the sides as this too will stop the layers of pastry being able to rise.) Lightly brush the smaller 8cm pastry lids with egg wash and gently score a criss-cross design onto each one.

Ingredients & method cont. overleaf

125g baby spinach, washed

50g plain flour

1 teaspoon medium curry powder

½ teaspoon ground turmeric

½ teaspoon black mustard seeds

400ml tin coconut milk

Juice of 1 lime

300g cooked peeled prawns

¼ bunch coriander, leaves picked and chopped

Fine table salt

Equipment

10cm and 8cm round pastry cutters

Place the tray in the preheated oven and bake both the pastry cases and lids for 20 minutes or until puffed and a deep caramel colour. Allow to cool for a few minutes.

While the pastry cases are cooking, prepare the filling. In a medium heavy-based saucepan, melt 30g of the butter with the vegetable oil. Add the onion, chilli and red pepper to the pan with a pinch of salt and sauté over a medium heat until soft; this will take around 6 minutes. Add the grated ginger and cook for 1 minute, then add the garlic and cook for a further minute. Toss in the baby spinach and sauté until just wilted, then transfer everything from the pan to a bowl and set aside.

Melt the remaining 50g of butter in the same pan, then stir in the flour, curry powder, turmeric and mustard seeds. Cook everything over a low heat for a few minutes. Pour in half of the coconut milk and whisk until there are no lumps and you have a smooth sauce. Add the remaining coconut milk and bring it up to a simmer. Season with 1 teaspoon of salt and the lime juice.

Return the spinach mixture to the pan and fold it back through the sauce, then stir in the prawns and chopped coriander.

These are best served immediately, so warm the prawns through then spoon the filling into the pastry cases. If any of the filling falls down the sides of the pastry cases, don't worry – I think this makes the prawn patties look even tastier. Top the prawn patties with the criss-crossed lids and serve immediately once filled.

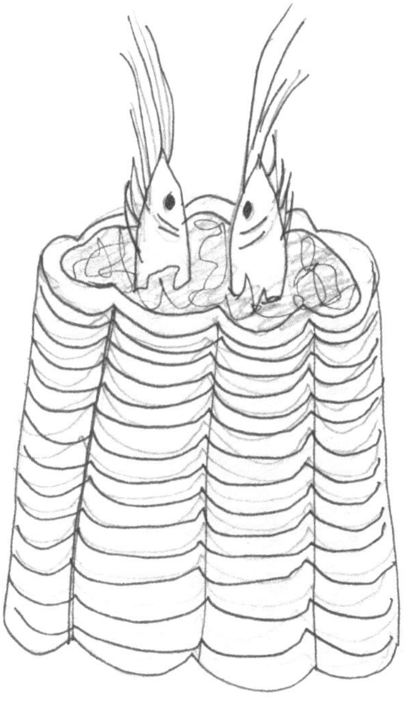

VINE'S ORIGINAL PRAWN PATTY GARNISHED WITH THE HEADS AND CURLY GREEN PARSLEY

Trawler Pie

The fish pie has been a long-present and ever-evolving dish within British food culture. There are written recipes for fish pies going back to the seventeenth century; some of the more flamboyant ones contained carp and eel, or hundreds of herrings that were baked in a pastry crust and sent to the king. The popularity of fish pie would rise with the observation of Lent, as ways were found to use up fish scraps and offcuts.

Recipes vary from stirring pre-cooked fish through a sauce to adding the fish raw and cooking it in the sauce. I have issues with both of these techniques. I find the former nearly always leads to overcooked fish and the latter usually results in a very wet final sauce as the fish releases moisture during cooking. As a happy medium, I have found that lightly curing raw fish draws out moisture before cooking so you have much more control over the sauce's consistency and things are less likely to go wrong later, plus it seasons the fish perfectly.

I always feel that a good Trawler Pie should be relatively simple: good fish, a tasty sauce and a crunchy mashed potato topping. Sometimes a recipe can feel like everything including the kitchen sink has been tipped into it and it loses that purity. I took out at least six unnecessary ingredients from this recipe before I was happy with this final version.

Serves 4

200g cod fillets, skin removed and cut into 3cm chunks

200g smoked haddock fillets, skin removed and cut into 3cm chunks

Sea salt, to cure the fish

110g butter

1 large Spanish onion, peeled and thinly sliced

1 head of fennel, trimmed and thinly sliced

3 tarragon sprigs, leaves picked and roughly chopped, stalks retained

400ml fish stock

90g plain flour

200ml double cream

Ingredients & method cont. overleaf

Method

Salt the cod and smoked haddock pieces with plenty of sea salt and leave on a plate in the fridge to cure for 15 minutes.

Meanwhile, melt 40g of the butter in a medium saucepan. Add the onion, fennel, tarragon stalks and 1 teaspoon of fine table salt and gently cook until the onion and fennel have softened fully. Pour in the fish stock and cook on a simmer until the liquid has reduced by a quarter. Strain off the liquid, setting aside the stock for the sauce. Remove and discard the tarragon stalks, and transfer the onion and fennel to a bowl. Leave aside.

Wipe the pan clean, then melt the remaining butter. Add the flour and cook out over a gentle heat for 3 minutes until just bubbling, stirring to stop it from burning. Add the reserved stock a few ladlefuls at a time, stirring until smooth. Repeat until all the stock has been incorporated. Add the cream and bring to a simmer, then turn off the heat. Fold in the grated Cheddar, stirring until smooth. Add the spring onions, capers, mustard, cayenne pepper, tarragon leaves, and lemon zest and juice. Taste the mixture to check the seasoning, adding a little more salt if needed.

100g mature Cheddar, grated

1 bunch spring onions, trimmed and thinly sliced

15g capers, finely chopped

2 teaspoons Dijon mustard

½ teaspoon cayenne pepper

Zest and juice of 1 unwaxed lemon

200g raw tiger prawns, shells removed

Fine table salt

For the topping

1kg Maris Piper potatoes, peeled and quartered

30ml milk

40g butter

1 egg yolk

30g Garlic Breadcrumbs (see page 258)

½ bunch chives, chopped

Equipment

24cm ovenproof dish

Potato ricer (optional)

Rinse the cured fish well, then pat dry with paper towels. Cut the prawns in half. Fold the fish and prawns into the mixture and then spoon it into the ovenproof dish. Set aside to cool a little while you make the potato topping.

Wipe clean the pan once more. Rinse the quartered potatoes under water until it runs clear, then put them in the pan. Add enough fresh water to just cover the potatoes and add enough salt so that the water is as salty as sea water. Bring the potatoes to a simmer and cook until they are soft throughout but not starting to absorb any water. Drain the potatoes in a colander and allow them to steam off for a few minutes.

Rinse out the pan again, then add the milk and butter. Warm until the butter is just starting to melt, then turn off the heat. Rice the potatoes into the milk and butter and beat together until smooth. (If you do not have a potato ricer, crush them really well with a potato masher.) Finally, fold in the egg yolk.

Preheat the oven to 190°C fan/210°C/gas mark 6½.

Spoon the potato topping on top of the filling and carefully smooth the surface flat. Drag a fork across the top of the potato layer to ruffle the surface.

Place the dish in the centre of the oven and bake the pie for 25 minutes. Remove the dish from the oven and scatter the breadcrumbs across the surface of the mash. Return the pie to the oven for a further 5 minutes.

When ready to serve, sprinkle chopped chives all over the top of the pie and enjoy with some steamed broccoli and lots of green peas dressed with butter and lemon juice.

FISH PIE DETAIL BASED UPON
CHRISTIAN LENT SYMBOLISM
FEB' 2024

Stargazy Pie

A dish deeply connected to the picturesque fishing village of Mousehole in Cornwall, it is said to have been created after storms cut off the region from the mainland and fisherman had to feed the population by braving the waters to bring in a catch. The Stargazy is said to celebrate Tom Bawcock, who took to those rough seas and came back with a haul of pilchards and mackerel that was turned into pies. The exact timing of all of this is slightly unclear but for 60 years it has been celebrated on the night of 23rd December in Mousehole. Known locally as Tom Bowcock's Eve, the village pubs serve Stargazys to punters on this day.

The original pies were filled with pilchards, with the heads and tails of some of the fish poking through the pastry crust, resembling the choppy waters that Bawcock braved. Whilst spectacular to look at, fish heads and tails are not usually eaten and therefore make the pie slightly impractical. The brilliant (and hilarious) chef, Elliott Grover, told me his story of cooking Stargazy Pie for a group of horrified chefs in LA; he got angry at them for not appreciating such an iconic piece of British food culture. But I get it. I wanted to find a way to honour the origins of this pie. I thought about it for a long time before concluding that the heads and tails could stay, I just needed to make them edible. Moreover, I needed make them so delicious that you would want to dip them in the sauce of the pie.

Serves 4

400g shortcrust pastry (see page 32, or shop-bought), or gluten-free shortcrust pastry (see page 36)

1 egg yolk, strained and beaten with 1 teaspoon water, for egg washing

8 white anchovies in vinegar (or marinated anchovies)

For the filling

90g butter

1 large Spanish onion, peeled and thinly sliced

1 head of fennel, halved and thinly sliced

Ingredients & method cont. overleaf

Method

In a wide-based pot, melt 40g of the butter over a medium heat. Add the onion and fennel and cook until softened; this will take about 4 minutes. Add the garlic, leeks and celery and cook for a further 3 minutes or until softened. Add the white wine and 1 teaspoon of salt, then cook until the wine has reduced.

In a medium saucepan, melt the remaining butter over a low heat. Add the flour and cook for 3 minutes, then add half the stock and cook until smooth. Pour in the remaining stock and warmed cream, then cook for 5 minutes. Stir in the lemon zest and juice.

Pour all of the sauce from the pan over the vegetables in the pot. Fold the vegetables through the sauce, then set aside. Stir in the smoked and raw mackerel along with the herbs. Set aside to cool to room temperature, then chill in the fridge.

Line a baking tray with parchment paper. On a lightly floured surface, roll out the pastry dough to a large square, 5mm thick. Slide the rolled-out pastry onto the lined tray and place in the fridge to chill for 15 minutes.

Cut out a 30cm circle from the middle of the pastry sheet. Retain the pastry trimmings and return them to the lined tray in the fridge.

2 garlic cloves, peeled and finely chopped

3 leeks, trimmed of the dark green tops, washed and thinly sliced

4 celery sticks, peeled and thinly sliced

100ml white wine

40g plain flour

350ml fish stock, warmed

100ml double cream, warmed

Zest and juice of 1 unwaxed lemon

140g smoked mackerel fillets, skinned and broken into large chunks

140g raw mackerel fillets, skinned and cut into large chunks

½ bunch chervil, roughly chopped (or if you cannot find chervil, use 2 tarragon sprigs)

½ bunch flat-leaf parsley, leaves picked

Fine table salt

Equipment

26cm ceramic pie dish

4cm and 2cm round pastry cutter

Using the tip of a sharp knife, score a fish scale pattern over the surface of the pastry. With a 2cm round pastry cutter, punch out four holes from the large pastry circle – I made four equally spaced holes around the pie (so every diner gets a pastry fish), making sure the holes are at least 6cm inside the outer edge.

Next, make a collar for each of the four holes out of the reserved pastry trimmings. Using a 4cm round pastry cutter, punch out four small discs and then push out the centre of those discs with the 2cm cutter to make a ring. Lightly brush a thin coating of egg wash around the holes in the pie lid, then position a ring around each hole to make a collar, gently pressing them in place.

Spoon the filing into the pie dish, making sure it is an even layer and the dish is no more than three-quarters full. Lightly brush the outside lip of the pie dish with the egg wash. Lay the large pastry circle across the top of the filling and dish, then gently press the overhanging pastry down onto the egg-washed lip to seal. Place the dish in the fridge and chill for 20 minutes to set hard.

Meanwhile, roll out the remaining pastry trimmings to half their original thickness, about 2.5mm. Cut eight identical fish shapes from the rolled-out pastry. I made mine around 8cm long and 2cm wide. If you include a tail on any of your fish shapes, make sure it is narrow enough to fit through the holes in the pie lid – if not, your fish will need to dive head-first into the pie when serving. Take one of the pastry fish shapes and lay two of the anchovies on top, stacking them one on top of the other. If necessary, trim the pastry so there is a narrow border of pastry all around the anchovies, then lightly brush the border with egg wash. Place another pastry fish on top of the anchovies and gently seal the two layers of pastry together. Repeat with the other pastry fish shapes and anchovies so you have four pastry fish. Place in the fridge and chill until needed.

Lightly brush the pie lid all over with a thin coating of egg wash. Add any further decoration that you like using any remaining pastry trimmings. Place the pie in the fridge and chill for 10 minutes.

Preheat the oven to 200°C fan/220°C/gas mark 7. Give the pie a light coating of egg wash then place in the centre of the oven and bake for 25 minutes.

While the pie is cooking, take the pastry fish from the fridge, trim them to neaten the edges and brush them all over with egg wash. Pop the pastry fish into the freezer for 10 minutes, then take them out, add a steam hole and score a few lines into the pastry on the tail ends. Place the pastry fish on a lined baking tray. When the pie has cooked for 25 minutes, place the tray in the oven and cook the pastry fish alongside the pie for a further 15 minutes.

When ready to serve, plunge the pastry fish either head-first or tail-first into the holes cut into the pie lid. Put the pie in the centre of the dining table alongside some boiled new potatoes and steamed broccoli.

Pastai Gocos

This Welsh recipe from the 1800s would have seen you soaking clams overnight in a mixture of oats and water, the idea being that the clams feed on the oats and clean themselves. (This was a task I was set as a young chef in restaurant kitchens, although I'm not sure this practice is common anymore.) The clams would then have been cooked, the meat removed from the shells and layered in a bowl with strips of bacon and chives, and finally topped with shortcrust pastry. Breaking open the pastry crust to be hit by the aromas of the clams would have been a magical moment. I wanted to achieve this same magic with my take on Pastai Gocos and so I thought of Paul Bocuse's famous truffle consommé created for a banquet at the Élysée Palace in 1975, which was topped with puff pastry. This is my interpretation of that moment via Wales. I have swapped bacon for chicken here so that the flavour of the clams is more prominent, but otherwise I have kept the recipe close to the original and as simple as possible.

Serves 4

500g inverse puff pastry (see page 46, or shop-bought puff pastry)

1 egg yolk, strained and beaten with 1 teaspoon water, for egg washing

For the filling

1kg fresh clams, soaked overnight in plenty of water and kept in the fridge

150ml white wine

50g butter

2 large brown onions, peeled and thinly sliced

2 garlic cloves, peeled and thinly sliced

1 litre chicken stock

Method

Drain the soaked clams. Remove and discard any clams that remain open or have damaged shells.

Heat a large, wide-based saucepan with a well-fitting lid over a medium heat. Pour in the white wine and bring to a simmer. Add the clams to the pan and pop on the lid on the pot, then turn the heat up to high. Cook the clams for 2 minutes, shaking the pan occasionally. Carefully remove the lid, avoiding any hot steam. If the clams have opened, turn off the heat. If the clams are still closed, put the lid back on and cook the clams for a further minute or so until they open. Remove and discard any clams that remain closed after cooking. Sit a colander over a bowl. Strain the clams in the colander, allowing the cooking juices to drain into the bowl. Set aside to cool a little.

In the same pan, melt the butter over a medium heat. Add the onions with a few pinches of fine table salt and, stirring continuously, cook for 5 minutes or until the onions have softened. Add the garlic, reduce the heat to low and cook for another minute while stirring. Pour in the chicken stock and reserved cooking liquid from the clams, then bring to a simmer. Add the chicken thighs and bring back to a simmer, then gently poach the chicken for 20 minutes.

Next, add the diced potato to the pan and cook for 8–10 minutes or until the potato is tender. Add the samphire at the last minute, just to soften.

Ingredients & method cont. overleaf

8 skinless chicken thighs on the bone

400g Maris Piper potatoes, peeled and cut into 1.5cm cubes

200g samphire (if you cannot find samphire, you can use young thin asparagus spears cut into 3cm pieces)

Zest of 1 unwaxed lemon

Fine table salt and ground white pepper

To serve

Creamed Leeks (see page 268)

Equipment

4 ovenproof soup bowls or mini casserole dishes

Sit the colander back over the bowl. Strain the chicken, potatoes, onions, garlic and samphire in the colander, catching the cooking liquid in the bowl. Set aside the chicken and vegetables to cool. Return the cooking liquid to the pan and set it over a medium heat to reduce the liquid by half. Taste to check the seasoning, adding a little salt, if needed, and ½ teaspoon of white pepper. Set aside.

Line a baking tray with parchment paper. On a lightly floured surface, roll out the pastry to a large square, 5mm thick. Slide the rolled-out pastry onto the lined tray. Place the pastry in the fridge to chill for 30 minutes.

Cut four large circles, each slightly larger all round than the top of your soup bowls or mini casserole dishes, from the sheet of pastry. Place on the lined tray and chill in the fridge while you continue to prepare the filling.

Once cool enough to handle, gently pick the cooked meat from the chicken bones, trying not to shred the meat too finely, then discard the bones. Pick the steamed clams out of their shells.

In a bowl, combine the chicken with the vegetables, then add the lemon zest and steamed clams. Divide the chicken and clam mixture evenly between the soup bowls or casserole dishes, then pour over the reduced cooking liquid, making sure they are no more than three-quarters full. Chill the soup bowls or casserole dishes in the fridge to room temperature.

Lightly brush the outside rim of each soup bowl or casserole dish with the egg wash, brushing about 3cm down the sides of the bowls. Lay a pastry circle centrally across the top of each bowl or dish; keeping the pastry taut, gently press the edges of the pastry against the egg-brushed rim all the way round. Lightly brush the pastry lid all over with a thin coating of egg wash. Return the bowls or dishes to the fridge and chill for a further 15 minutes. (It is important that the soup bowls or casserole dishes and the filling are either room temperature or cold at this point, otherwise the pastry will melt.)

Preheat the oven to 200°C fan/220°C/gas mark 7.

Brush the pastry lids with a final thin coating of egg wash. Being very careful not to cut all the way through the dough, gently score the pastry with a decorative design – I made a series of intersecting parallel lines to create a diamond effect.

Place the bowls or dishes on a baking tray in the centre of the preheated oven and bake for 20 minutes or until the pastry is puffed and a deep caramel colour.

Serve with some creamed leeks alongside.

Yorkshire Christmas Pie

Enjoyed by British royalty and US presidents – it was a favourite of both Queen Victoria and George Washington – the Yorkshire Christmas Pie is steeped in tradition. Recipes for the pie go back to the eighteenth century, the most famous of which is probably Hannah Glasse's from *The Art of Cookery, Made Plain and Easy*; given that her recipe included six different birds, 2kg of butter and a lot of flour, that was a slightly misleading title. Filled with game birds, chicken, turkey and many other ingredients, the pie was a huge, ornate pastry structure assembled by teams of cooks in large stately kitchens and then shipped to London to be eaten during the festive period. Glasse wrote: 'These pies are often sent to London in a box, as presents; therefore, the walls must be well built.' Given the size of the pies, it was likely in these earlier recipes that the pastry was beautiful but inedible. Documented in the *York Chronicle*, I found reference to one made in late December of 1835: 'On Thursday was baked at the Bakehouse of Mr Severs, Leeds, a tremendous Christmas Pie containing thirteen tongues, two geese, four fowls, ham, four rabbits, two hares, two pheasants, half a stone of veal, two stones of pork – and weighing upwards of thirteen stones.' Now that's a lot of tongue.

You will be relieved to know my version of this pie is not quite as complex and yet is just as impressive; it fits inside a domestic oven, is entirely edible and doesn't require a team of cooks (perhaps just a small team of guests to eat it). If you want to do this recipe full justice, don't skip the blanching stage of the filling: this sets the ballotine of rolled meats into a neat cylindrical shape and gives a beautiful cut-through. To do this, you need a large stockpot that is at least 30cm in diameter, which is pretty big. If you want to skip the blanching stage, it's not the end of the world – the final product will still look great – however, the chef in me pines for perfection. Also, a temperature probe is definitely needed here. If you haven't got one, it's a solid investment with many uses. I advise buying one with an ovenproof cord, which you can close the oven door on, so you can keep the probe in the pie during cooking rather than continually taking the pie out of the oven to check its temperature. Allow yourself a generous amount of time to make this pie. You could split the making over two days by prepping the meat on day one, storing it overnight in the fridge, and then encasing the meat in the pastry, decorating and baking the pie on day two. The end result will be incredibly rewarding and a talking point amongst guests for years after; nobody really remembers a roast turkey.

Ingredients & method overleaf

Serves 6–8

- 200g Cumberland pork sausagemeat
- 200g merguez lamb sausages, skins removed
- 80g dried apricots, roughly chopped
- 2 rosemary sprigs, needles picked and finely chopped
- 80g panko breadcrumbs
- ½ teaspoon ground white pepper
- 4 boneless chicken thighs
- 2 duck breasts
- 500g turkey breast
- 30 slices (around 150g) bresaola
- 1kg shortcrust pastry (see page 32, or shop-bought), or gluten-free shortcrust pastry (see page 36)
- 2 egg yolks, strained and beaten with 2 teaspoons water, for egg washing
- Fine table salt

Equipment

- Large stockpot (at least 30cm in diameter and 20cm deep)
- Digital temperature probe
- Round pastry cutters

Method

In a large bowl, combine the Cumberland pork sausagemeat, lamb merguez sausages, chopped apricots, rosemary and panko breadcrumbs with the ground white pepper and 1 teaspoon of salt. Set aside until needed.

Remove any skin and sinew from the chicken thighs. Using a rolling pin, flatten them between a folded sheet of parchment paper, giving them a few good whacks so they flatten properly; you want them to be no more than 1cm thick. Season the chicken evenly with a few pinches of salt. Set aside.

Remove any skin and sinew from the duck breasts. Slice each breast lengthways into four strips. Season the duck evenly with a few pinches of salt and set aside with the chicken thighs.

Remove any skin from the turkey breast. Without slicing all the way through, make horizontal cuts into the turkey breast to open it up like a book. Flatten the turkey in the same way as the chicken thighs. Season the turkey with a few more pinches of salt and set aside with chicken thighs and duck breasts.

Lay a large 50 × 40cm rectangle of clingfilm on your work surface. Using a clean dish towel, working from the middle to the outside edges, smooth out the clingfilm to remove any air bubbles. Lay a second layer of clingfilm directly on top of the first, then smooth it out as before.

Working from the bottom edge of the clingfilm closest to you, lay out the bresaola slices into a 30 × 25cm rectangle, slightly overlapping the slices. There should be a clear border of clingfilm along the top and down both sides of the bresaola.

Starting at the bottom edge, but leaving a gap of 5cm along the top and 3cm down each side of the bresaola, lay the flattened turkey breast evenly across the sliced meat in a 24 × 20cm rectangle.

Flatten out two-thirds of the sausagemeat between parchment paper so it is 20 × 17cm. Leaving a 3cm border of turkey clear along the bottom edge, lay the sausagemeat on top of the turkey.

Next, lay the chicken thighs on top of the sausagement, starting about 2cm up from the bottom edge of the sausagemeat; the chicken thighs should form a rectangle roughly 20 × 15cm.

Flatten out the remaining sausagemeat as before, then lay it across the chicken thighs, starting just a few centimetres up from their bottom edge.

Finally, lay the duck strips evenly across the middle of the last layer of sausagemeat, gently pressing them into the meat.

Lift the clingfilm along the bottom edge and use it to roll up everything into a large, tight parcel with the bresaola encasing all the other meat. As you start the roll, take care to keep the clingfilm out of the centre of the roll; instead neatly tuck in the ends of the bresaola. As you complete the roll, the clear border of excess bresaola along the top edge will roll onto the length of the parcel to seal everything in. Gently tuck in the excess bresaola at each end. Making sure no clingfilm is caught anywhere in the bresaola and without trapping any air, finish by gently wrapping the meat parcel completely in the clingfilm, folding over the ends to ensure it is airtight.

Once everything is neatly rolled, lay the meat parcel down onto some fresh clingfilm and wrap tightly. This will compress the parcel into a neat barrel shape. Tie off each end to make sure no air can get in.

If blanching the meat parcel, fill a large, wide stockpot with enough water to cover the parcel and bring it up to a simmer. Carefully lower the parcel into the pot, turn off the heat and leave for 20 minutes. Drain the water from the pot, then re-fill it with ice-cold water to chill the meat. Leave to cool for at least 45 minutes. This extra step ensures an attractive roulade shape, but it is not essential, so if you do not have pot large enough, skip straight to rolling out the pastry. Just be sure to unwrap and handle the meat parcel very gently as it will be softer.

Line a large baking tray with parchment paper. On a lightly floured surface, roll out two-thirds of the pastry to a 45 × 35cm rectangle, 5mm thick. Roll out the remaining dough to a 35 × 25cm rectangle, also 5mm thick. Trim away any excess pastry. Slide the rolled-out pastry onto the lined baking tray and place in the fridge to rest for at least 30 minutes. Save any pastry trimmings for decoration, so transfer those to the lined tray too and rest in the fridge.

Remove the smaller rectangle of pastry from the fridge and lay it on a sheet of parchment paper. Carefully remove the clingfilm from the chilled meat parcel using sharp scissors, taking care not to snip into the bresaola wrapping. Lay the meat parcel directly on the pastry so there is a clear border all around it. Lightly brush this pastry border with the egg wash.

Remove the larger rectangle of pastry from the fridge and allow it to become pliable. Working quickly and confidently to avoid making tears, lay the pastry directly over the meat parcel, aligning the corners and edges with the egg-washed border below. Try to avoid making any pleats or creases the dough. If you work along the length of the parcel, from one end to the other, you can nudge out any air pockets before pressing down on the pastry dough to fully seal it against the egg-washed border of the base. Slide onto a lined baking tray and chill for 20 minutes in the fridge.

Method cont. overleaf

Lightly brush the pie all over with the egg wash. Using the reserved pastry trimmings, add any decoration you like. I added four wide strips of pastry decorated with a repeating scales pattern, draped over the pie at a slight angle. I then added three leaf shapes at either end. As a finishing touch, I made a plait from two thin ropes of pastry and then ran that around the base of the pie. Make three small holes evenly spaced along the top of the pie, using a small round pastry cutter, to allow any steam to escape during cooking. I like to make small rings from a thin rope of pastry that are the same size as the steam holes and place them on top. Either run a pastry cutter around the bottom border to create a wave effect or crimp in the edges of the borders towards the pie. Chill the pie again for a further 15 minutes.

Preheat the oven to 190°C fan/210°C/gas mark 6½.

Give the whole pie a final egg wash, making sure the crimped border and all the decoration has an even coat. Push the end of the digital probe thermometer directly into the middle of the meat parcel and place the pie in the preheated oven. Once the temperature probe reads 30°C, turn the baking tray around 180 degrees to make sure that the pie cooks evenly. When the temperature probe reads 53°C, take the pie out of the oven. The internal temperature of the pie will keep rising during the resting time and go well above 63°C, so it will be safe to eat but crucially not dry. Allow the pie to rest for 30 minutes before slicing with a serrated knife. Serve with all the usual Christmas accompaniments – I also like to serve it with Pease Pudding (see page 269) and Braised Red Cabbage (see page 257).

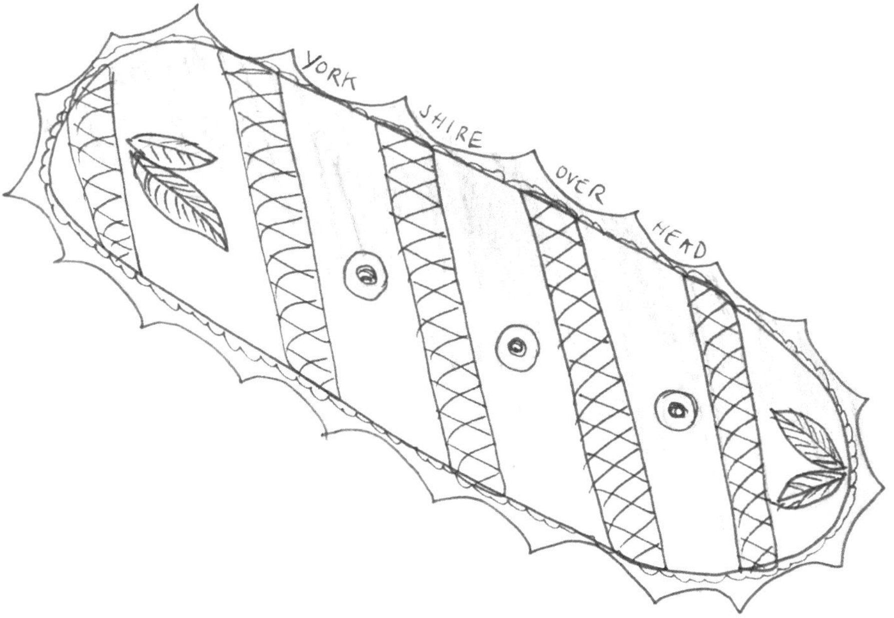

ENJOYED BY

British royalty

AND

US PRESIDENTS

THE YORKSHIRE CHRISTMAS PIE

is steeped in tradition

Balti Pie

A pie born out of the Midlands, this is one of my all-time favourites. Whilst studying at University College Birmingham, the now Head of Department at The College of Food there, Lewis Walker, and I were in digs together and regularly ended up in very late-night balti houses after big nights out. These pies remind me of that really special time in my life. It wasn't much before my university days when balti cooking emerged in 1970s Birmingham, apparently created as a way to appease the British palate of the time. Its roots are in Pakistani-Kashmiri cooking and the base of the curry always has to contain tomatoes, onions, peppers and chillies, although variations can be built on those foundations. It's a wonderful celebration of multicultural Britain.

Enjoyed on football terraces across the nation, the first Balti Pie is thought to have been served at Walsall Football Club in 1977. They are now sold at over 60 football grounds throughout the UK. There is a version of the Balti Pie that not many know (or have considered) outside of the UK, but it is the stuff of dreams… The Balti Pie Barm: a whole Balti Pie inside a soft bread roll. Don't knock it until you have tried it.

Serves 4

- 6 chicken thighs on the bone
- 1 teaspoon medium curry powder
- 1 teaspoon garam masala
- ½ teaspoon ground turmeric
- ½ teaspoon chilli powder
- ½ teaspoon ground cumin
- ½ teaspoon ground cinnamon
- 70g butter
- 1 red onion, finely chopped
- 1 green pepper, deseeded and cut into small cubes
- 1 garlic clove, peeled and chopped
- 2cm piece of ginger, peeled and chopped

Ingredients & method cont. overleaf

Method

Preheat the oven to 190°C fan/210°C/gas mark 6½.

Place the chicken thighs in a roasting tray and season with a pinch of salt. Place the tray in the oven and roast the chicken for 25 minutes and cooked through, then set aside to cool.

Lower the oven temperature to 185°C fan/205°C/gas mark 6.

Scatter all the ground spices over a sheet of foil. Place the foil in the oven and toast the spices for 10 minutes. (Turn the oven off.)

Meanwhile, melt 50g of the butter in a wide-based pan. Add the red onion, green pepper, garlic and ginger and cook over a low heat until softened.

Add the toasted spices to the pan with the vegetables and cook for a minute, then add the chopped tomatoes, tomato purée and chicken stock. Bring everything to a simmer over a medium heat and reduce the sauce by half. Turn off the heat.

When cool enough to handle, strip all the meat off the chicken bones and chop into small nuggets.

In a small bowl, mix a tablespoon of cold water into the cornflour to make a slurry, then stir that into the sauce. Stirring continuously, bring the sauce gently back up to a simmer. Add the chopped chicken, mixing it well, then add the lime zest and juice. Taste to check the seasoning, adding a little salt if

400g tin chopped tomatoes

1 teaspoon tomato purée

200ml chicken stock

1 heaped tablespoon cornflour

Zest and juice of 1 lime

10g fresh coriander, roughly chopped

16 frozen roti paratha

1 egg yolk, strained and beaten with 1 teaspoon water, for egg washing

Pinch each of nigella seeds and fennel seeds, for topping

Fine table salt

To serve

Spicy Green Chutney (see page 251)

Equipment

Non-stick 12-hole muffin tray

needed. Finally, fold through the chopped coriander. Set aside to cool to room temperature, then chill in the fridge.

Grease eight of the holes in the muffin tin with the remaining butter. Take the paratha out of the freezer. Working swiftly as the paratha defrost quickly, roll out eight of the paratha to about 11cm. Line each hole in the muffin tin with a rolled-out paratha and fill them about three-quarters of the way with the balti mixture. Lightly brush the exposed paratha with a little water. Use the remaining paratha to close off the pies, gently crimping the edges together but don't worry about being too neat – I like to give them a rustic look. Chill the pies in the fridge for 15 minutes.

Preheat the oven to 200°C fan/220°C/gas mark 7.

Using a sharp knife, make a small hole in the top of each pie. Lightly brush the top of each pie with a thin coating of egg wash and scatter the nigella and fennel seeds across the tops of the pies.

Place the muffin tray in the oven and bake the pies for 30 minutes. Serve immediately while hot, with some green chutney for dipping.

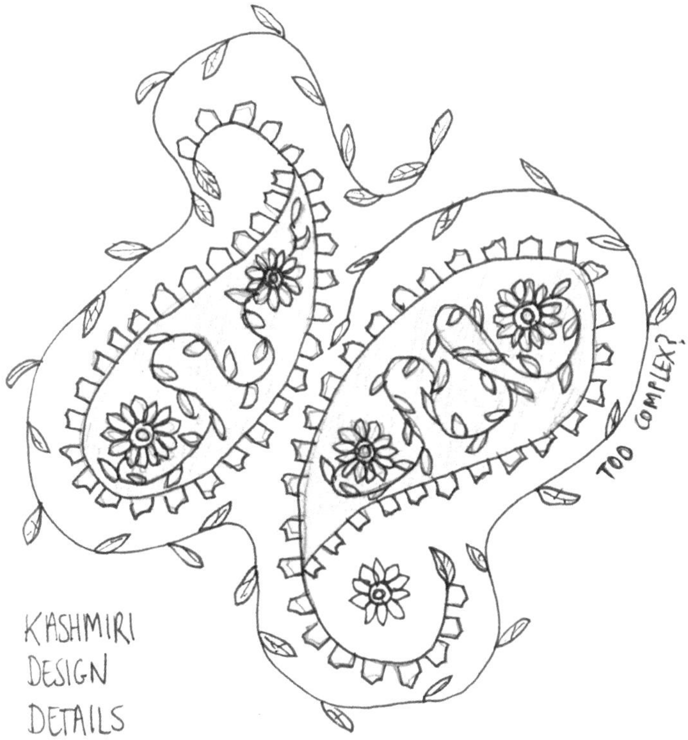

Quail Timbales

A timbale is a drum-shaped mould that was used to create tall, cylindrical pies. In Victorian times, the use of small game birds was commonplace, with teal, snipe and woodcock being featured regularly on celebration tables. These pies were petite, structured and often elegant. I first came across them in Frederick T. Vine's book, *Savoury Pastry*, from 1900. Sold by the Brockley pie maker in his shops, they would have been equally at home on the table of a royal banquet, too.

If you are not confident in small bird surgery, ask your butcher to remove the quail meat for you – just make sure that they give you everything to take home as you will need the carcass to make the gravy. My version of this traditional pie has the quail sandwiched between mushroom duxelles and roasted chestnuts, which both sit very well alongside the sweet quail meat.

Serves 4

800g shortcrust pastry (see page 32, or shop-bought), or gluten-free shortcrust pastry (see page 36)

1 egg yolk, strained and beaten with 1 teaspoon water, for egg washing

For the filling

4 whole quails

30ml vegetable oil, plus extra for greasing

500g chestnut mushrooms, roughly chopped

30g butter

2 banana shallots, peeled and finely chopped

1 garlic clove, peeled and finely minced

80g cooked chestnuts, roughly chopped

Ingredients & method cont. overleaf

Method

Skin the quails and remove the breasts and legs (or ask your butcher to do this; see recipe introduction).

Preheat the oven to 180°C fan/200°C/gas mark 6 and line a roasting tray with foil.

Place the quail carcasses and legs in the lined tray. Place the tray in the oven and bake the carcasses and legs for 20 minutes. After 20 minutes, remove the legs and set aside to rest. Return the tray to the oven and continue cooking the carcasses for a further 10 minutes.

Place the roasted carcasses in a medium saucepan and pour over the chicken stock. Bring up to a simmer, add the honey and sherry vinegar, then continue cooking until the stock has reduced by half. Sit a colander over a bowl. Strain the quail carcasses in the colander, and allow the stock to drain into the bowl. Discard the carcasses, then return the stock to the pan.

In a small bowl, mix a tablespoon of cold water into the cornflour to make a slurry, then whisk that into the stock. Whisking continuously, bring the stock gently back up to a simmer for 1 minute, then turn off heat. Taste to check the seasoning, adding a little salt if needed. Set aside until ready to be reheated and served with the timbales.

Heat the oil in a large, wide-based pan over a high heat. Add the mushrooms with a few pinches of salt, then cook until any liquid released by the mushrooms has totally evaporated. Once the mushrooms have taken on a little colour, turn off the heat.

- 4 thyme sprigs, leaves picked
- 200g large leaf spinach, washed
- Fine table salt and freshly ground black pepper

For the gravy

- 500ml chicken stock
- 1 tablespoon honey
- 1 teaspoon sherry vinegar
- 1 heaped tablespoon cornflour

To serve

Slow-roasted root vegetables

Equipment

Four 120ml pudding basins or large teacups of a similar size

In a separate pan, melt the butter over a low heat. Add the shallots, garlic and chestnuts until cook until the shallots have softened, then add the thyme leaves. Scrape the chestnut mixture into the pan with the mushrooms. Add a few twists of black pepper and taste to check the seasoning, adding a little salt if needed. Set aside.

Preheat the oven to 170°C fan/190°C/gas mark 5 and line a baking tray with foil.

In batches, lay the spinach leaves over the foil-lined tray, making sure they do not overlap. Place the tray in the oven and bake the spinach for 1–2 minutes or until just wilted. Lay a clean, dry dish towel on your work surface, then place the spinach on the towel, this time overlapping the leaves to make a 30cm square. Repeat until you have cooked all the spinach and laid them out in 30cm square with no gaps. Lightly press the spinach down onto the towel to remove any remaining moisture.

Lightly grease the inside of the basins or teacups with a little vegetable oil. Tear off a sheet of clingfilm that is about 40cm square and lay it flat on your work surface. Using a clean dish towel, working from the middle to the outside edges, smooth out the clingfilm to remove any air bubbles. Lay a second layer of clingfilm directly on top of the first, then smooth it out as before. With one horizontal cut and one vertical cut, divide the double layer of clingfilm into four equal squares. Line each basin or cup with one of the clingfilm squares, using a dish towel to push the clingfilm right down into the base. The edges of the clingfilm should overhang the rim of the basin or cup, and this will be used to unmould the filling later.

Using a sharp knife, divide the layer of spinach into four equal squares. Carefully line each basin or teacup with one of the spinach squares. Again, the edges of the spinach should overhang the rim.

Split the mushroom and chestnut mixture in half. Divide one half of the mixture evenly between the four lined basins or cups, gently pressing down with the back of a spoon.

Place the quail breasts between a folded sheet of parchment paper. Using a rolling pin, gently tap the breasts to thin them out to the dimensions of the basin or cup. Season the meat with a few pinches of salt. Place two of the quail breasts into each basin or cup, carefully nudging them down onto the mushroom and chestnut mixture, keeping them flat and even. Top the quail breasts with the remaining mushroom and chestnut mixture, pressing it down with the back of a spoon. Bring the overhanging spinach from the sides over the centre to make a neat parcel. Place the basins or cups in the fridge to chill while you roll out the pastry.

Line a large baking tray with parchment paper. On a lightly floured surface, roll out two-thirds of the pastry dough to at least 40cm square, 5mm thick. Roll out the remaining dough to a square, also 5mm thick. Slide the rolled-out pastry onto the lined tray. Place the tray in the fridge to chill for 20 minutes.

Cut out four 20cm circles from the larger sheet of pastry and set aside.

From the smaller sheet of pastry, cut out four 12cm circles and sit them on a sheet of parchment paper. Turn out the moulded quail, mushroom and chestnut fillings onto the centre of each 12cm pastry disc, removing the basin or cup and clingfilm. Lightly brush the clear border of pastry around the filling with a thin coating of egg wash.

Once the 20cm pastry discs are pliable, lay one over the top of each filling. Gently nudge the pastry disc down the filling. When you have covered three-quarters of the filling with the pastry, make sure there is no trapped air under the pastry before continuing so the outer edges meet the egg-washed border of the pastry case, avoiding any creases or folds in the dough. Seal the final section of the filling with the pastry. Gently press the joined pastry around the base to make sure the two layers of pastry are joined. Transfer the pies to a lined baking tray, lightly brush all the pastry with a thin coating of egg wash, then chill in the fridge for 15 minutes.

Preheat the oven to 200°C fan/220°C/gas mark 7.

Lightly brush the pies with a final thin coating of egg wash, then tidy up the edges of the bases either with a large round pastry cutter or a sharp knife. Using a skewer or the tip of a knife, make a small hole in the top of each pie to allow the steam to escape.

Place the tray in the centre of the oven and bake the pies for 35 minutes, turning them 180 degrees halfway through the cooking time. Remove from the oven and rest the pies for 5 minutes before serving.

When ready to serve, reheat the quail gravy. Serve the timbales with the gravy and lots of slow-roasted root vegetables.

Wiltshire Lattice

Hailing from the South West of England, the unique wrapping of this sausage roll-like pie makes it easily identifiable as a Wiltshire Lattice. Here the addition of caramelised onion and yeast extract brings depth to the flavour with a welcome umami note. Traditionally the pastry would have been a lard-based, hot water crust pastry, which gave way to shortcrust in later years. For me, however, puff pastry is far better suited to this pie, and more enjoyable to eat.

Serves 4–5

800g rough puff pastry (see page 44, or shop-bought puff pastry)

1 tablespoon yeast extract (I use Marmite)

1 egg yolk, strained and beaten with 1 teaspoon water, for egg washing

For the filling

20ml vegetable oil

1 large brown onion, peeled and thinly sliced

1.2kg Cumberland pork sausagemeat

6 sage sprigs, leaves picked and finely chopped

80g panko breadcrumbs

Fine table salt and ground white pepper

Equipment

Lattice pastry cutter roller

Method

In a medium pan, heat the vegetable oil over a medium heat. Add the onion with a few pinches of table salt and, stirring continuously, cook until any liquid released by the onion has evaporated. Turn down the heat to low and cook until the onion is well caramelised and a deep toffee colour – this will take around 15–20 minutes. If the onion is sticking or catching, add a splash of water to the pan. Transfer the caramelised onion to a plate and set aside to cool.

Line a large baking tray with parchment paper. Divide the pastry dough into equal halves. On a lightly floured surface, roll out each half to a 15 × 35cm rectangle. Slide the rolled-out dough onto the lined tray. Place the tray in the fridge and chill the pastry for at least 30 minutes.

Once cool, roughly chop the caramelised onion. In a bowl, mix the chopped onion through the sausagemeat along with the chopped sage, 1 teaspoon of salt and ½ teaspoon of ground white pepper. Add the panko breadcrumbs to the bowl, lightly crushing them between your hands as you add them, then combine everything well.

Tear off a sheet of parchment paper. Across the centre of the sheet, form the sausage mixture into a thick log shape around 6cm in diameter. Using the paper, shape the mixture into a neat roll – imagine rolling some tobacco in cigarette paper to make a cigarette. Try to keep the thickness to around 6cm and the length to a maximum of 30cm. Set aside.

Take one of the chilled pastry sheets and lay it flat on your work surface. Place the lattice pastry cutter roller at one end of the pastry, centering it on the dough. Whilst lightly trapping the very end of the dough with your palm, roll the pastry cutter up to the other end of the dough to cut out the lattice lengthways. Keep the roller in a straight line and apply a good amount of pressure as you roll. Slide the pastry back onto the lined tray and pop it back in the fridge for 10 minutes.

Method cont. overleaf

At this point, I like to ensure that the lattice is properly cut and each cut has gone all the way through the pastry so it opens up nicely when stretched. To do this, slowly and methodically go over each small cut made by the roller with a sharp knife. If the pastry is getting warm at any point, just pop it back into the fridge (or even better the freezer).

Take the second pastry sheet and, leaving a clear border of 3cm all the way round the edges, lightly brush the pastry with the yeast extract. Place the shaped sausagemeat directly down onto the yeast extract-brushed dough.

Lightly brush the clear 3cm border of pastry around the sausagemeat with the egg wash. Take the pastry lattice and gently ease it out, stretching the strip until the lattice is evenly spread over the top of the sausagemeat, like a net. Align the edges of the lattice with the egg-washed edges of the pastry base, then push this part down to flatten slightly and join together the two layers. Lightly brush the joined pastry with a thin coating of egg wash, then crimp this border of pastry back towards the sausagemeat. Place the whole lattice in the fridge and chill for at least 15 minutes.

Preheat the oven to 200°C fan/220°C/gas mark 7.

Apply one final thin coating of egg wash to all the exposed pastry. Place the tray in the preheated oven and bake the lattice for 35 minutes or until the pastry is golden all over.

Remove from the oven and serve warm in thick wedges before serving warm with some sliced pickled walnuts.

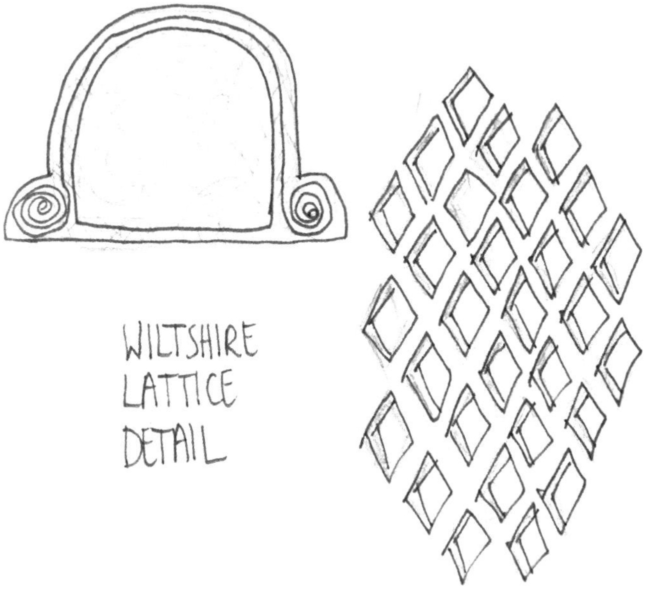

Ploughman's Pork Pie

This is not necessarily a historic pie in itself, rather it is a marriage of two beautiful British food traditions: the cold pork pie and the ploughman's lunch. The plump pickled onions running down the centre of the pie act as a foil to the rich pork filling and crumbly pastry. It is a good-looking picnic pie with the jellied top – something I think that Ian Heircock, Master Pie Maker of Walker & Sons and all-round pie legend, would enjoy. In some ways, this recipe is a small tribute to him as a thanks for all the knowledge, tips and tricks he has given me over the years.

Serves 4–6

400g hot water crust pastry (see page 43)

10g softened butter, for greasing

1 egg yolk, strained and beaten with 1 teaspoon water, for egg washing

For the filling

750g pork shoulder, minced (or pork mince with 20% fat)

200g cooked ham hock, flaked

150g smoked bacon lardons

100g lardo, cut into 1cm dice

50g panko breadcrumbs, blitzed or crushed to fine crumbs

50g shelled pistachios, roughly chopped

Ingredients & method cont. overleaf

Method

Line a baking tray with parchment paper. On a lightly floured surface, roll out the pastry to a large rectangle, about 35 × 25cm, 5mm thick. Slide the rolled-out pastry onto the lined tray. Chill in the fridge for 20 minutes.

Grease the insides of the loaf tin with the butter. Lay a strip of parchment paper along the base of the tin, allowing the ends to overhang the sides. (This will help to remove the pie from the tin once cooked.)

Take the pastry sheet and make a 7cm diagonal cut from each corner towards the centre of the sheet (see page 20). Drop the pastry into the greased tin – the cuts will allow you to tuck the pastry easily and neatly into the tin. Trim away any excess dough from the corners of the tin where the edges overlap. Make sure the dough is in good contact with the bottom of the tin, then gently work up the sides and into the corners, making sure the seams in the corners are fully sealed without any holes. Chill in the fridge for 10 minutes.

In a large bowl, combine the pork shoulder, ham hock, lardons, lardo, panko, pistachios, fennel seeds, mustard seeds, lemon zest, sage and 2 teaspoons of salt, then mix together until well combined.

Preheat the oven to 200°C fan/220°C/gas mark 7.

Divide the pie filling equally into two halves. Put the first half into the pastry-lined loaf tin, packing it down. Arrange the pickled onions in a line down the centre of the tin, pressing them down slightly. If using shop-bought baby

1 teaspoon fennel seeds, lightly toasted

1 teaspoon yellow mustard seeds

Zest of 2 unwaxed lemons

30g sage leaves, finely chopped

10 Beer-Pickled Baby Onions (see page 255, or 8 shop-bought baby pickled onions)

Fine table salt

For the jelly

3 bronze gelatine sheets

150g redcurrant jelly

100g dried cranberries

Handful of tarragon leaves

To serve

Green salad leaves

Cheddar

Crisps

Equipment

900g (2lb) non-stick loaf tin

Digital probe thermometer

pickled onions, trim a little off each end to get a more uniform channel of onions. Cover the pickled onions with the remaining pie filling, gently packing the mixture down.

Trim any excess pastry overhanging the top of the tin back to 2cm and neatly crimp it down onto the edges of the meat. Lightly brush the pastry with a thin coating of egg wash. Cut a rectangle of parchment paper that fits neatly over the surface of the pie filling and then stick it down.

Bake in the preheated oven for 25 minutes. Remove the paper from the top of the filling, lower the temperature to 185°C fan/205°C/gas mark 6 and cook for a further 20 minutes. Insert a digital probe thermometer into the centre of the pie: if it reaches 65°C, take the pie out of the oven; if not, leave the pie in for a little longer and check again. The internal temperature of the pie will rise above 73°C while it rests. Leave to cool, then chill the pie in the fridge overnight (still in the tin).

Soak the gelatine sheets in ice-cold water. Meanwhile, warm the redcurrant jelly in a small pan until it melts. Add the dried cranberries to the jelly and cook for 2 minutes over a gentle heat. Squeeze the excess water from the gelatine and melt it into the jelly.

Pour this jelly mixture over the top of the pie, trying not to get any over the crimp of the pastry or down the edges of the pie. Lay the tarragon leaves inside the jelly, distributing them evenly, then leave to set. Allow to chill for 2 hours in the fridge before taking the pie out of the tin.

To serve, place the pie on a board or large platter and cut into slices with a serrated knife. Serve with a light green salad, a thick wedge of Cheddar and lots of good-quality crisps.

Pork Pie

There have been Pork Pie comparisons drawn between recipes going as far back as the first century AD, with some food historians looking later at the spectacular *The Forme of Cury* written by King Richard II's master cooks in 1390 for the Mylates of Pork recipe, which was more akin to a modern-day quiche than a pie. For me, it is not until we reach at least an edible pastry crust that we get close enough to the Pork Pie that we know so well in Britain for any comparisons to be valid.

The Pork Pies of the sixteenth and seventeenth centuries were simpler beasts. The pastry and cold jelly that encased the meat filling are still there as a form of preservation for lengthy horseback journeys; heavy spicing, fruits and sugars are used to mask any unwanted flavours after long travel. However, it was not until the nineteenth century that these flavours fell away to leave the more savoury pies of cured meat and fats that we are accustomed to now.

The Pork Pie has many variations. Probably the best known is the Melton Mowbray, a style protected by European Protected Designation of Origin status since 2009. To be called a Melton Mowbray pie means it must be made within 28 square kilometres of the town and with uncured pork. These types of pies are traditionally raised by hand around a pie dolly, which is a small wooden tool around which the dough is shaped into a cup to be filled with the pork. The meat is cut by hand rather than minced. The pies are then baked without any support, which gives the pastry its signature bowed shape. My retail pie partners, Dickinson & Morris, started making this style of Pork Pie back in 1851 and if you are looking for an authentic example, they are the best out there by a country mile. (Yes, I know. Of course I would say this, but it is honestly true.)

This interpretation of the classic Pork Pie is a large, sharing pie; designed to feed a group of friends, it makes a beautiful centrepiece on the dining table when entertaining. One thing I really like about making a Pork Pie in a larger format is that it gives the pastry longer to cook, which in turn will last longer and stay crisper after cooking.

Serves 6

- 700g hot water crust pastry (see page 43)
- 10g softened butter, for greasing
- 1 egg yolk, strained and beaten with 1 teaspoon water, for egg washing

Ingredients & method cont. overleaf

Method

Place the ham hock in a medium saucepan and cover with cold water. Add the carrots, onion, garlic, cloves and sage stalks and simmer over a low heat for around 2½ hours until the meat comes away from the bone, topping up the water whenever necessary to ensure the meat stays submerged. Remove the ham hock from the pan and set aside to cool. (You can speed up the cooling process by breaking up the ham hock meat.)

Increase the heat and reduce the stock left in the pan by half. Strain the stock through a fine-mesh sieve into a clean pan or jug, leave to cool to room temperature and then store in the fridge until needed for the jelly. Discard the vegetables and aromatics, although I like to snack on the carrots as a chef's perk – they are delicious!

For the filling

1 ham hock

2 carrots, peeled and halved

1 large Spanish onion, peeled and quartered

3 garlic cloves, lightly crushed

30g sage sprigs, leaves picked and finely chopped, stalks reserved

750g pork shoulder, minced

200g smoked bacon lardons

150g lardo, cut into 1cm dice

50g panko breadcrumbs, blitzed or crushed to fine crumbs

50g peeled pistachios, finely chopped

1 teaspoon fennel seeds, lightly toasted

1 teaspoon yellow mustard seeds

Zest of 2 unwaxed lemons

Fine table salt

For the jelly

2 bronze gelatine leaves

150ml ham hock stock (reserved from cooking the ham)

While the ham hock is cooling, roll out the pastry. First, line a baking sheet with parchment paper. On a lightly floured surface, roll out two-thirds of the dough to a large 35cm circle, 5mm thick. Repeat with the remaining dough, rolling it out to about 22cm in diameter, so there is a small border overhanging the edges of the tin when placed on top of the pie base. Reserve any pastry trimmings to be used later for decoration. Slide the rolled-out pastry and trimmings onto the lined baking sheet and place in the fridge to chill for 20 minutes.

Next, grease the tin with the butter. Drop the larger pastry circle into the tin and press the dough onto the base and sides, making sure the dough goes all the way into the edges and without any creases or folds anywhere. Trim the pastry overhanging the rim of the tin back to 2cm all the way round. Put the pastry-lined tin in the fridge to chill until needed.

In a large bowl, combine the pork shoulder, lardons, lardo, panko breadcrumbs, pistachios, fennel seeds, mustard seeds, chopped sage leaves, lemon zest and 2 teaspoons of salt, then mix well. When the ham hock is cool, chop the meat roughly and work it into the mixture without shredding it down.

Take the pastry-lined tin from the fridge and fill with the pie filling, packing it down. Lightly brush the overhanging pastry around the top of the tin with a little water. Place the smaller pastry circle over the top of the pie filling without pressing it down onto the meat. (A little gap is a good thing.) Gently pinch together the two layers of overhanging pastry back to a thickness of 5mm. Trim back this overhanging pastry to leave a neat 3cm border all the way round.

Lightly brush the surface of the pie with a thin coat of egg wash. Crimp the overhanging pastry up and over onto the top of the pie (see page 25). Put it back into the fridge to chill for 15 minutes.

Using a sharp knife, score any decoration onto the lid of the pie. I made a delicate feather design. Using a 2cm round pastry cutter, make a hole in the centre of the pie lid. Cut a collar from the pastry trimmings to sit around the hole. (I use a 4cm round pastry cutter and punch a hole out of the centre with the 2cm cutter.) Lightly brush the pie again with a little egg wash, then position the collar around the hole. Brush the collar with egg wash, especially on the edges where it touches the pie lid as this will stop it rising off the surface. Tear off a small piece of foil and fold it in half. Curl the folded tin foil around the 2cm cutter, then slide the cutter out to leave a foil cylinder – you want the cylinder to be about 3–4cm tall. Make the foil cylinder a tiny bit tighter, then fit it into the steam hole in the top of the pie. Egg wash just at the base of the foil cylinder where it touches the pastry collar. In the oven, as the pastry cooks, it will seal in the foil cylinder to make a working chimney. (Any juices released

To serve

English mustard

Beer-Pickled Baby Onions (see page 255) or your choice of pickles

Equipment

20cm round springform cake tin

Digital probe thermometer

Small round pastry cutters

during cooking will travel up the chimney and then go back down into the pie as it cools, so you don't lose any moisture or flavour. Otherwise, the juice will leak onto the pastry, all over the top of the pie, and burn.

Preheat the oven to 200°C fan/220°C/gas mark 7.

Bake in the preheated oven for 20 minutes. Turn the oven temperature down to 185°C fan/205°C/gas mark 6 and cook for a further 25 minutes. Insert the digital probe thermometer through the foil chimney and push it down halfway into the meat filling to read the core temperature. Once it reads 65°C, remove the pie from the oven. The temperature will continue to rise to above 70°C while the pie rests. Remove from the oven and allow to cool to room temperature on a wire rack and then refrigerate overnight.

The next day, make the jelly. In a small bowl, soak the gelatine leaves in cold water. Meanwhile, warm the 150ml of ham hock stock reserved from the day before. Once the gelatine leaves are soft, dissolve them in the hot stock.

Remove the foil chimney from the pie whilst being careful not to damage the pastry collar around the steam hole. Slowly pour the jelly mixture through the hole to fill the pie. If the jelly mixture leaks from any point, pop the pie back into the fridge for 10 minutes and the jelly should set and block the hole. Once any holes are blocked, continue until the pie is fully filled with the jelly mixture. Chill the pie in the fridge for at least 1 hour before serving so the jelly is fully set.

To serve, cut large wedges and eat ideally as part of a picnic with some good mustard and your choice of pickles.

PORK PIE DETAIL

Hoggan Pies

An indicator of the economic landscape of Cornwall over time, the Hoggan was seen as the inferior, cheaper version of a Cornish pasty, as it was made from dough left over from the pasty-making process. In even harder times the pastry would be replaced with barley bread containing a little meat and potato to make it as inexpensive as possible: the Hoggan pie became more about survival and nourishment.

This version pays respect to the simplicity of the Hoggan, with the addition of a little mustard to liven things up. The pork filling releases its own juices to create a delicious sauce inside the pie.

Serves 4

- 800g hot water crust pastry (see page 43)
- 1 egg yolk, strained and beaten with 1 teaspoon water, for egg washing

For the filling

- 400g Maris Piper potatoes, peeled and cut into 2cm dice
- 450g pork tenderloin, sinew removed and cut into 2cm chunks
- 1 tablespoon cornflour
- 1 bunch spring onions, top 1cm of green trimmed and discarded, the rest finely sliced
- 1 heaped tablespoon wholegrain mustard
- Fine table salt and freshly ground black pepper

Method

Line a baking tray with parchment paper. Divide the dough equally into 4 balls. On a lightly floured surface, roll out each ball into a 20cm circle, 5mm thick. Slide the rolled-out pastry onto the lined tray, with more sheets of parchment paper between the pastry circles, and rest in the fridge for 20 minutes.

Place the potatoes in a small saucepan, cover with cold water and add a few good pinches of salt. Bring to a simmer and cook until just tender, then drain and set aside to cool.

In a large bowl, combine the pork with 10g of fine table salt and mix well. Leave to sit for 5 minutes so the salt draws out some of the moisture from the pork. Sprinkle in the cornflour and toss to coat the pork. Finally, mix in the spring onions, mustard and ½ teaspoon of black pepper, then fold through the potatoes.

Arrange the pastry circles evenly spaced on the baking tray and spoon a quarter of the pork mixture in the centre of each one, shaping it into an oval and stopping about 1cm from each side. Lightly brush the exposed areas of dough on just one side with egg wash. Bring both sides of the pastry up and over the filling and pinch together to seal. Squeeze the crimp between your index finger and thumb, about 3cm apart, then use the index finger of your other hand to go between in opposite direction and create a wave-shaped crimp (see page 25).

Lightly brush the pies with a thin coating of egg wash over all the exposed pastry. Chill in the fridge for 20 minutes. Meanwhile, preheat the oven to 200°C fan/220°C/gas mark 7.

Give each pie a final thin coat of egg wash, then make a small hole at the top on one of the sides to allow the steam to escape. Bake in the centre of the oven for 40 minutes or until the internal temperature measures 65°C or above on a digital probe thermometer. Allow the pies to cool for 10 minutes then serve.

Bedfordshire Clanger

Found in the south Midlands and South East of England, clangers are still eaten regularly today. Reflecting its humble beginnings, liver and onions were wrapped in suet dough and steamed in a muslin cloth. Shortcrust dough has now taken precedence, as I have used here. Clangers were often taken by wives to their husbands working in the fields for lunch. The name 'clanger' could have originated from local dialect 'clung', which meant heavy in relation to food, but similarly 'clanger' may have referred to the noisy eating of the pastry.

The two halves of a clanger – yes, there is a savoury side and a sweet side – didn't come about until the twentieth century; before then it was a purely savoury pie. There are versions now, such as the clangers you can buy at Gunns bakeries in Bedford and the surrounding areas, where the meat and the fruit are separated by a pastry 'dam'. I have omitted that dam in my recipe because there is something magical that happens in that crossover area where the apple meets the salty pork and sage. I think it's probably the best bit.

Serves 3–4

- 800g shortcrust pastry (see page 32, or shop-bought), or gluten-free shortcrust pastry (see page 36)
- 1 egg yolk, strained and beaten with 1 teaspoon water, for egg washing

For the apple filling

- 2 large cooking apples, peeled, cored and cut into 1cm dice
- 1 Granny Smith apple, peeled, cored and cut into 1cm dice
- 1 teaspoon ground cinnamon
- 20ml apple cider vinegar
- 2 tablespoons light brown soft sugar

Method

First prepare the apple filling. Put the apples, cinnamon, vinegar, soft brown sugar, lemon zest and juice together with 20ml water into a medium saucepan with a lid. Cover with the lid and cook, stirring occasionally, over a medium heat until the cooking apples have started to break down and the Granny Smith apple has softened. Transfer the cooked apple to a bowl and set aside to cool.

Next prepare the pork filling. Wipe out the pan, then add a little vegetable oil and warm over a medium heat for 1 minute. Add the onion and carrots and cook until softened, around 4–5 minutes. Using a slotted spoon, transfer the vegetables to paper towels to remove any oil.

Place the sausagemeat, rosemary, panko and 1 teaspoon of salt in a bowl, then mix in the onion and carrots. Grind in lots of fresh black pepper and set aside until needed.

Line a baking tray with parchment paper. On a lightly floured surface, roll out two-thirds of the dough into a circle 5mm thick. Cut a 35cm circle from the rolled-out dough and slide onto the lined tray.

Repeat with the remaining one-third of the dough, cutting out a 25cm circle and sliding it onto the tray. Place some of the pastry trimmings on the tray to use later for decoration. Roll the rest of the scraps into a ball. Place the rolled-out pastry in the fridge to chill for 20 minutes.

Ingredients & method cont. overleaf

Zest and juice of
1 unwaxed lemon

For the pork filling

Vegetable oil

1 large Spanish onion, peeled and finely diced

3 medium carrots, peeled and finely diced

300g Cumberland pork sausagemeat

4 rosemary sprigs, needles picked and finely chopped

20g panko breadcrumbs, lightly crushed

Fine table salt and freshly ground black pepper

To serve

Braised Red Cabbage (see page 257) or single cream

Equipment

20cm savarin mould

6cm round pastry cutter

Lightly grease the savarin mould with a little vegetable oil. Tear off a large sheet of clingfilm and use it to line the mould. (The clingfilm will be used to remove the pie from the tin.) Rest the centre of the 35cm pastry disc over the raised middle section of the mould and let it drop in and drape down into the sloped inner sides of the ring, then nestle it back up the outer sides. Using the ball of scraps, nudge the pastry into the walls of the mould, avoiding any folds or creases. There should be roughly 2cm of pastry overhanging the edge of the tin – do not trim it off.

Stuff the sausagemeat filling into one half of the mould and the apple filling into the other half. Using a marker pen, note on the tin where the meat ends and the apple begins. (When you flip it over, the marks will help you identify exactly where the fillings are.)

Lightly brush all the exposed dough with a little water. Lay the 25cm pastry disc on top of the mould and gently press the edges of the pastry layers together to seal in the fillings. Flip the mould over onto a tray lined with parchment paper. Using the marker pen, note on the paper where the two fillings start and finish inside the clanger. Carefully remove the mould, using the clingfilm to ease the tin from the pie.

Using the round pastry cutter, punch out a hole from the centre of the ring. Press the remaining dough in the centre of the ring until it is very thin, then lightly tuck it under the inner edges of ring to make the centre hole slightly larger.

Lightly brush the pie all over with a thin coat of egg wash. Crimp the overhanging border of pastry around the outer edge up and onto the ring of the pie (see page 25), then add any decoration. I added some uniform leaf shapes, but you could add two distinct styles of decoration that indicate where the two fillings are inside the pie – for example, from the pastry, cut a small apple shape to decorate the sweet side and a pig's nose to indicate the savoury side. Chill in the fridge for 20 minutes.

Preheat the oven to 200°C fan/220°C/gas mark 7.

Apply one more thin coating of egg wash all over the pie. Using a metal skewer, poke several small holes into the top of the ring to allow steam to come out during cooking.

Bake the pie in the oven for 40 minutes, then remove from the oven and allow to rest for 10 minutes.

Serve thick slices of the pie with some braised red cabbage to accompany the sausagemeat side and some single cream for the apple side.

Gala Pie

An offshoot of the pork pie family tree, the Gala Pie is very similar in structure until you reach the centre where you will find treasure – a perfectly cooked egg. Well, that is the theory. My memories of this pie from childhood (and most of my adult life, to be honest) are of a slightly doughy, grey meat surrounding a slightly overcooked, grey boiled egg that seemed to be staring into my soul; I couldn't ever see the attraction.

Around ten years ago, I had a revelation: the egg wasn't staring at me, it was pleading to be cooked nicely. So I set about finding the correct technique to achieve cooked pastry, cooked meat and soft egg yolks all at the same time. After some considerable time, I cracked it. This version of Gala Pie is the latest and best iteration of that journey. It makes for a really spectacular slice of pie and is absolutely worth the effort. There are parts of the UK where Gala Pie is known as Grosvenor Pie, but the filling remains the same in both. Whatever it is called, I'm a fully paid-up fan of this pie now.

Serves 4

- 700g shortcrust pastry (see page 32, or shop-bought), or gluten-free shortcrust pastry (see page 36)
- 1 egg yolk, strained and beaten with 1 teaspoon water, for egg washing

For the filling

- 4 large eggs, at room temperature
- 30g butter
- 1 large Spanish onion, finely chopped
- 1 teaspoon fennel seeds, lightly toasted
- 600g Cumberland pork sausagemeat

Ingredients & method cont. overleaf

Method

Bring a large pan of water to the boil. Carefully lower the eggs into the boiling water with a spoon, making sure you don't crack them on the base of the pan, and cook for 6½ minutes (if you cook them for any longer, then you won't have beautifully soft yolks). Meanwhile, fill a large bowl with iced water and keep it close by. Remove the eggs from the pan using a slotted spoon and plunge them straight into the iced water to stop them cooking any further. Leave the eggs to cool for at least 20 minutes. Once cool enough to handle, carefully peel the shells from the eggs. Refill the bowl with fresh cold water and store the eggs in the bowl in the fridge until needed.

Line a large baking tray with parchment paper. On a lightly floured surface, roll out two-thirds of the dough to a 30 × 22cm rectangle, 5mm thick. Roll out the rest of the dough to a 25 × 12cm rectangle, also 5mm thick. Reserve any trimmings to be used later for decoration. Slide the rolled-out pastry onto the lined tray and chill in the fridge, along with the trimmings.

Melt the butter in a frying pan over a low heat. Add the onions and fennel seeds and gently cook until soft, around 5 minutes. Set aside to cool.

In a bowl, combine the sausagemeat, ham, figs, panko breadcrumbs, sage, lemon zest, 5g of fine table salt and a few twists of black pepper, then mix together with your hands until well combined. Knead in the cooked onions and fennel seeds.

Tear off a sheet of clingfilm and lay it on the work surface. On the clingfilm, flatten out the sausagemeat mixture into a 20 × 12cm rectangle, making sure it is even and level. One third of the way along the long side of the rectangle,

150g cooked ham, cut into 1cm dice

100g dried figs, roughly chopped

40g panko breadcrumbs, blitzed to fine crumbs

20g sage leaves, finely chopped

Zest of 1 unwaxed lemon

Fine table salt and freshly ground black pepper

To serve

Cabbage, steamed or boiled

Spiced Brown Ketchup (see page 250)

Chunky Piccalilli (see page 256)

Equipment

Digital probe thermometer

Small round pastry cutter

make a small channel across the sausagemeat – the eggs will line up in this channel so they are suspended in the very centre of the meat.

Using a sharp knife, trim a thin slice (about 5mm) off the very top and bottom of each boiled egg. Sit the eggs in the channel in the pie filling, lining them up end to end. Using the clingfilm, lift and roll the sausagemeat over the eggs so that the sides of the pie filling join up and encase the eggs. Tuck in the overlaps at each end and wrap the whole thing in the clingfilm to make a neat sausage shape. Gently tighten the clingfilm to achieve a smooth, even shape, but don't squeeze too hard otherwise the eggs may break!

Slide the smaller pastry rectangle onto a sheet of parchment paper. Lay the sausage in the centre of the pastry, unwrapping it from the clingfilm, and leaving a narrow but even border of pastry all the way round. Lightly brush the exposed border of pastry with a thin coat of egg wash. Gently shape the sausagemeat with your palms so the bottom is flat and in contact with the dough while the top is still rounded or domed (imagine the entrance to a train tunnel).

Take the other larger pastry rectangle from the fridge and allow it to become malleable, then lay it over the top of the sausagemeat, joining it up with the border of egg-washed pastry and trying not to capture any air bubbles. Gently press the pastry layers together where they join at the base to thin them out a little. Trim the border back to 3cm to neaten. Lightly brush the pastry all over with a thin coat of egg wash. Crimp the pastry border inwards towards the pie. Chill in the fridge for 20 minutes.

Preheat the oven to 200°C fan/220°C/gas mark 7.

Using the reserved pastry trimmings, decorate the pie. I cut some very thin lengths of pastry and draped them over the pie to make six slightly angled lines. I then cut and scored three leaf shapes that I placed in three of the spaces defined by the lines. Finally, I used the small round pastry cutter to make two holes in the spaces not decorated with a leaf, then made a thin collar or ring of pastry to sit around each hole. Even if you choose not to decorate the pie, make a couple of small holes in the top of the pie to allow the steam to escape during cooking. Give everything a final coat of egg wash.

Bake in the preheated oven for 40 minutes. Insert the digital probe thermometer into the centre of the pie through one of the small steam holes; when the pie reaches 60°C, remove from the oven and leave to rest. The core temperature will keep rising during the resting period.

If eating hot, allow the pie to rest for 15 minutes, then slice and serve with boiled or steamed cabbage and spiced brown ketchup. If eating cold, chill the pie overnight and serve slices with piccalilli and spiced brown ketchup.

Fidgit Pie

This triumph of a pie is a joy to cook. Traditionally made with gammon, cider, potatoes, onions and apples, it is certainly a handsome collection of ingredients that sit well alongside each other.

With its origins in Shropshire dating back 400 years, and with close cousins including versions from Derbyshire and Huntingdon, there are a few theories on the naming of the pie. My favourite fidgit theory is that it was often five-sided (fitched). Others are that the rather roughly cut, thick slices of ingredients fidgeted around inside the pie. Then there is the slightly less palatable idea that as the pie cooked, it smelled of polecat (locally known as fitchett). As I tested versions of the Fidgit Pie in my home oven to lovely aromas, I did think to myself that polecat must be pretty tasty in that case.

Some more modern versions of this pie, especially in Ludlow, have a mashed potato topping instead of pastry. However, I prefer a full pastry case as it allows for the pie to be served either hot or cold and is equally appetising in both cases.

During recipe testing, I found that whilst the potato and apple can be left fairly thickly cut, the gammon should really be sliced quite thinly for a better structure inside the pie. The amount of gammon used stays the same, but it makes slicing much neater.

Serves 6

800g shortcrust pastry (see page 32, or shop-bought), or gluten-free shortcrust pastry (see page 36)

2 egg yolks, strained and beaten with 1 teaspoon water, for egg washing

For the filling

200ml dry cider

100ml semi-skimmed milk

200ml double cream

6 rosemary sprigs, needles picked and finely chopped

1kg Maris Piper potatoes, peeled

Vegetable oil

Ingredients & method cont. overleaf

Method

Put the cider, milk, cream and rosemary into a large saucepan with 20g fine table salt and bring up to simmer. Turn off the heat and leave to infuse.

Meanwhile, thinly slice the potatoes (about 2–3mm thick) using either a sharp knife or mandolin. Add the potatoes to the pan and mix together well.

Preheat the oven to 180°C fan/200°C/gas mark 6.

Line the baking dish with parchment paper. Arrange the potato slices in the dish in layers, then pour over the liquid. Cover with another sheet of parchment paper.

Cook in the preheated oven for 30 minutes, then lower the temperature to 160°C fan/180°C/gas mark 4. Turn the dish 180 degrees in the oven and cook for a further 35 minutes. Remove from the oven and allow to cool to room temperature on a wire rack, then chill in the fridge.

Divide the pastry dough into three balls weighing 400g, 250g and 150g. Tightly wrap each one in clingfilm and flatten slightly before putting into the fridge to rest for 20 minutes.

Meanwhile, in a heavy-based pan, heat a little vegetable oil, then cook the onions with a pinch of salt over a low heat until soft and translucent. Set aside to cool.

2 large Spanish onions, peeled and thinly sliced
2 Pink Lady apples
600g gammon, thinly sliced
Fine table salt

To serve

Mushy Peas (see page 271)
Green salad leaves
English mustard

Equipment

25cm round baking dish
900ml pudding basin
Lattice roller

Line a baking tray with parchment paper. On a lightly floured surface, roll out each of the balls of dough to a circle, 5mm thick. Slide them onto the lined tray with more parchment paper between them to stop the pastry sticking and return to the fridge. Leave to rest for 15 minutes.

Turn out the baked potato slices onto a chopping board. Cut out a circle to the same dimensions as the pudding basin, then cut that in half horizontally to give two thin discs.

Peel and core the apples, then thinly slice them.

Line the pudding basin with clingfilm (rubbing a little olive oil inside the basin can make it easier).

Layer some of the remaining potato trimmings in the bottom of the lined pudding basin, then add a layer of apple slices, a layer of onions and a layer of sliced gammon, lightly packing down each layer. Repeat these layers until the potato trimmings are used up, then move onto using the two thin discs of potato and continue layering until the pudding basin is full. (I usually manage to make three or four layers of each ingredient.)

Line a baking tray with parchment paper. Put the medium pastry circle on the lined tray and turn out the pie filling from the basin onto the centre, leaving an even clear border of pastry all the way round.

Lightly brush the border of pastry with a little egg wash. Drape the large pastry circle over the filling and, taking care not to trap any air bubbles, gently press together the two layers of pastry around the bottom of the pie to seal. Lightly brush the pie all over with a thin coat of egg wash. Place in the fridge to chill for 10 minutes.

Take the small pastry circle and use the lattice cutter roller to make the pastry lattice.

Remove the pie from the fridge and check the egg wash; after 10 minutes, it should be just tacky to the touch. Stretch out the pastry lattice and drape it over the pie. Gently push it down to cover the pastry top of the pie, then firmly press down around the bottom to seal. Finally, crimp in the edges of the pie to secure the base of the lattice (see page 25). Chill in the fridge for 30 minutes.

Preheat the oven to 190°C fan/210°C/gas mark 6½.

Lightly brush the pie all over with a thin coat of egg wash. Bake in the oven for 45 minutes, turning the pie 180 degrees in the oven halfway through the cooking time.

Either serve the pie immediately while hot with mushy peas or later at room temperature with a light salad and a good dollop of English mustard.

Cheshire Pork Pie

Despite its name, this is a dish that has little in common with the classic cold pork pie. Rather this is a superb hot pie that can be found in Hannah Glasse's eighteenth-century cookbook, *The Art of Cookery, Made Plain and Easy*. Glasse made excellent use of pork, potatoes and 'Pippins' apples, plus the pie was quite heavily spiced, as was the fashion at the time. Interestingly, her book was exported to North America after its publication and heavily influenced colonial cookery there, so the Cheshire Pork Pie can still be found in parts of America, including Virginia and Massachusetts. In the UK it is much scarcer nowadays, which I feel is a shame as it is such a classic.

The recipe I give here uses slow-cooked pork shoulder, rather than the traditional loin, which dries out somewhat in cooking. Light additions of a few herbs and a little mustard both layer in a bit of extra flavour.

Serves 6

800g shortcrust pastry (see page 32, or shop-bought), or gluten-free shortcrust pastry (see page 36)

10g softened butter, for greasing

1 egg yolk, strained and beaten with 1 teaspoon water, for egg washing

For the filling

30g butter

1 brown onion, peeled and thinly sliced

600g pork shoulder, rind/skin removed and cut into 3cm dice

Method

Preheat the oven to 160°C fan/180°C/gas mark 4.

Melt the 30g of butter in a saucepan over a medium heat. Add the onion with a pinch of salt and cook for 5 minutes or until soft.

Place the diced pork shoulder in a bowl and sprinkle over 10g of fine table salt; rub the salt into the meat. Add the salted pork and pancetta to the pan with the onion and cook for a few minutes until the pork is no longer pink and raw. Pour in the stock and bring up to a simmer. Transfer everything to an ovenproof casserole dish and cover with the lid.

Place the casserole dish in the centre of the oven and bake for 2½ hours.

Meanwhile, line a baking tray with parchment paper. Divide the dough into two balls: one weighing 500g and the other 300g. On a lightly floured surface, roll out the 500g ball into a circle, 5mm thick. Slide this onto the lined tray. Roll out the 300g ball also to 5mm thick and cut out a 26cm circle. Reserve any pastry trimmings to be used for decoration later. Slide the rolled-out pastry and trimmings onto another sheet of parchment paper and rest it on top of the first circle. Chill in the fridge for 35 minutes.

Ingredients & method cont. overleaf

70g smoked pancetta, diced

1 litre chicken stock

250g new potatoes, halved

2 cooking apples, peeled, cored and roughly diced

1 heaped tablespoon cornflour

1 tablespoon Dijon mustard

3 rosemary sprigs, needles picked and finely chopped

Fine table salt and ground white pepper

Equipment

Ovenproof casserole dish with a lid

24cm springform cake tin

Grease the insides of the springform cake tin with the softened butter. Line the tin with the larger pastry circle (see page 18), making sure to press the dough all the way into the corners and sides. Trim back any excess pastry overhanging the top of the tin to 3cm. Chill in the fridge until the pork filling has cooked and cooled.

Carefully remove the lid from the casserole dish and add the potatoes and apples. Replace the lid and cook for a further 35 minutes. Remove the casserole dish from the oven, take off the lid and allow to cool for a few minutes. Turn off the oven.

In a small bowl, make a slurry with the cornflour and a tablespoon of cold water. Quickly stir the slurry into the pork mixture along with the Dijon mustard, rosemary and ½ teaspoon of white pepper. Set aside to cool to room temperature.

Fill the pie case with the pork mixture. Lightly brush the exposed border of pastry overhanging the rim of the tin with a little water. Place the smaller circle of pastry on top to form a lid, aligning the edges of the circle with the pastry collar. Lightly brush the surface of the pie lid with egg wash, then crimp the now-joined overhanging border over onto the pie lid (see page 25). (Do not allow the crimp to protrude further than the rim otherwise it will be difficult to remove the pie from the tin.)

Using the reserved pastry trimmings, add any decoration you like. I cut out three large leaf shapes and lightly scored them with lines, which I then arranged over the pie top. Chill the pie in the fridge for 20 minutes.

Preheat the oven to 200°C fan/220°C/gas mark 7.

Give the pie a final thin coat of egg wash, then make a small cross or hole in the centre of the lid to allow the steam to escape.

Bake in the oven for 45 minutes or until the internal temperature reaches at least 65°C on a digital probe thermometer. Remove from the oven and rest the pie for 10 minutes before removing it from the tin and sliding it onto a serving plate.

Serve the pie while hot, sliced into wedges, with some steamed green vegetables.

THE **Thought** OF IT ON pub menu boards across Britain, **SCARING** THE LIFE OUT OF *tourists*, really rather **appeals** TO *Me*

Buckinghamshire Bacon Badger

Closely related to the Bedfordshire Clanger (and the Trowley Dumpling), the Buckinghamshire Bacon Badger has roots going back to the nineteenth century. Originally bacon, potatoes and onions (no badger) were steamed in suet pastry, although sometimes roasted. It was a heavy affair that took hours in the oven. It is a dish that is rarely seen anymore, but I do hope this pie makes a comeback – the thought of it on pub menu boards across Britain, scaring the life out of tourists, really rather appeals to me.

My interpretation is closer to the roasted version seen in twentieth-century recipes and has a little more structure with the addition of sausagemeat. I hope I have done the badger proud.

Serves 4–5

600g shortcrust pastry (see page 32, or shop-bought), or gluten-free shortcrust pastry (see page 36)

1 egg yolk, strained and beaten with 1 teaspoon water, for egg washing

For the filling

400g Maris Piper potatoes, peeled and quartered

250g smoked streaky bacon, cut widthways into 5mm strips

150g smoked pancetta, diced

100g cooked ham hock, shredded

1 tablespoon Dijon mustard

Method

Place the potatoes in a saucepan and cover with cold water, then add a few good pinches of salt. Bring to a simmer and cook the potatoes until just tender, around 15 minutes. Drain the potatoes in a colander and leave to cool.

In a large, dry frying pan, cook the bacon and pancetta over a medium heat until brown and crispy. Drain off any excess fat and add them to a bowl along with the cooked potatoes, shredded ham hock, Dijon mustard and lemon zest. Mix all the ingredients together in a bowl, lightly crushing the potatoes.

Line a baking tray with parchment paper. On a lightly floured surface, roll out the dough to 5mm thick and cut out a 40 × 25cm rectangle. Reserve any pastry trimmings to be used for decoration later. Slide the rolled-out pastry onto the lined tray and rest in the fridge for 25 minutes (or 15 minutes in the freezer).

In a bowl, combine the sausagemeat with the panko breadcrumbs, sage and ½ teaspoon of white pepper, then mix together with your hands until well combined. Spread the sausagemeat mixture lengthways over one half of the pastry – the channel of meat should be about 6–7cm wide and 30cm long – leaving a 3cm clear border of pastry at the edges and plenty of pastry on the other half to fold over the top of the meat (like a sausage roll). Spoon the potato mixture on top of the sausagemeat and shape it into a dome along the length (imagine the entrance to a train tunnel).

Ingredients & method cont. overleaf

Zest of 1 unwaxed lemon

600g Cumberland pork sausagemeat

30g panko breadcrumbs

4 sage sprigs, leaves picked and finely chopped

Fine table salt and ground white pepper

To serve

Spiced Brown Ketchup (see page 250)

Equipment

Small flower-shaped pastry cutters (optional)

Lightly brush the 3cm border of pastry all around the filling with a thin coat of egg wash. Fold over the other half of the pastry to cover the sausagemeat, aligning the edges of the dough. Gently press the two layers of pastry together along the joined edges, being careful not to trap any air bubbles beneath the pastry. Chill in the fridge for 20 minutes.

Using a sharp knife, make small diagonal cuts into the border of pastry along the top, bottom and one long side. Brush all the exposed pastry with a light coat of egg wash and add any decoration to the top of the pie. I lightly scored the top of the pie with criss-cross lines to make a diamond pattern, then punched out ten small flower shapes using a cutter, which I spaced evenly down the length of the pie. Even if you choose not to decorate the pie, make a couple of small holes in the top of the pie to allow the steam to escape during cooking. Give the pie a final thin coat of egg wash. Chill for a further 10 minutes.

Preheat the oven to 200°C fan/220°C/gas mark 7.

Bake in the preheated oven for 40 minutes or until the internal temperature reaches at least 65°C on a digital probe thermometer. Remove from the oven and allow to rest at room temperature for 10 minutes.

Serve slices with some spiced brown ketchup and a mug of tea.

BUCKINGHAMSHIRE BACON BADGER DETAILS '25

Norfolk Plough Pudding

Celebrations heralding the ploughing of spring crops, usually on the first Monday after Epiphany, date back to the fifteenth century in the UK. At what were nationally quite raucous events, village customs included all sorts of merriment: lots of drinking, costume processions and parades of Plough Monday Mummers, who took around actual ploughs as a threat to dig up the gardens of those who did not donate money to the village.

The Plough Pudding was invented in Norfolk around the early beginnings of these celebrations. I imagine it would have been something substantial and necessary to sustain revellers during the drinking and partying. Sadly, Henry VIII put an end to much of the Plough Monday customs by outlawing 'plough lights' from being displayed in churches in the mid-sixteenth century under the Reformation, which led to further restrictions over time. However, it often takes more than that to stand in the way of a good party in the UK; some local parades continued through until the nineteenth century, with a full-blown revival in the twentieth century.

The Norfolk Plough Pudding is a pork sausagemeat, bacon, onion and sage filling steamed inside a suet pastry crust. In testing I found that the richness of that filling, whilst delicious, could be overly heavy, so I added the zest of a lemon and some toasted fennel seeds into one and it just lifted it slightly. The lemon zest also enhances the flavour of the sage, which gives a little more complexity to the ingredients sitting alongside each other. Traditionally the pudding is served straight out of the steaming basin, but I found that resting it for 30 minutes and then turning it out of the basin and baking it in a hot oven for 10 minutes keeps the juices within the filling on slicing and allows the pastry to go a little crusty on the outside, which is a textural delight when eating.

Serves 4

800g suet pastry (see page 49)

10g softened butter, for greasing

For the filling

20g unsalted butter

2 brown onions, peeled and finely diced

Method

Make the suet pastry no more than 2 hours before baking (as the raising agent in the self-raising flour needs to activate during steaming). Once made, flatten the suet pastry dough and chill in the fridge for at least 45 minutes (but no more than 2 hours) before using.

While the suet pastry is chilling, melt the 20g of butter in a medium saucepan over a medium heat. Add the onions and cook until soft and translucent, about 10 minutes. Set aside to cool.

Grease the insides of the pudding basin with the 10g softened butter.

Ingredients & method cont. overleaf

500g Cumberland pork sausagemeat

200g smoked bacon lardons

Zest of 1 unwaxed lemon

1 tablespoon finely chopped sage

1 teaspoon fennel seeds, lightly toasted

Fine table salt and freshly ground black pepper

To serve

Roasted, steamed or boiled pointed cabbage

Your choice of gravy

Equipment

500ml pudding basin

Once the suet pastry has rested, roll it out on a lightly floured surface to 7–8mm thickness. Cut out a large circle that is twice the size of the circumference of the basin. Drop the pastry circle into the basin and gently press the dough against the sides of the basin, taking care not to trap any air. Leave any excess pastry overhanging the edges. Place the basin in the fridge (or freezer, if the basin is freezer-safe and you have space) until needed.

Meanwhile, cut another circle from the rolled-out pastry – re-rolling the trimmings, if necessary – this time to the same size as the inner rim of the basin. Slide onto a sheet of parchment paper and place in the fridge until needed.

In a large bowl, combine the sausagemeat, lardons, lemon zest, sage, fennel seeds and the cooked onion. Season with 10g fine table salt and plenty of freshly ground black pepper.

Fill the pastry-lined basin to the rim with the sausagemeat mixture, then lay the pastry circle over the top. Lightly brush the outer edges of the pastry circle with a little water, then carefully fold the overhanging excess pastry on top. Gently press the two layers of pastry together.

Cut out a circle of parchment paper large enough to cover the exposed dough and place on top of the basin. Tear off a large square of foil and make a 3cm overlapped fold down the centre of the foil. Tightly wrap the top of the basin with the foil. (The overlapped fold in the foil will allow for the pie to expand during steaming.)

Place the basin in a large pot with a lid and pour in enough water to come three-quarters of the way up the sides of the basin. Bring the water to a simmer and then set a timer for 3 hours. Put the lid on the pot and leave the pudding to steam, checking every now and then to make sure the water is still simmering, rather than boiling, and topping up the water level to make sure it is maintained.

Using a heatproof cloth or gloves, carefully remove the basin from the pot and let it rest for 30 minutes. Meanwhile, prepare and cook some pointed cabbage and make a gravy.

Preheat the oven to 200°C fan/220°C/gas mark 7.

Remove the pudding from the basin and blast it in the oven for 10 minutes to get a crust on the outside of the pastry. Transfer the pudding to a wide serving dish and serve portions of the pudding with the cabbage and a jug of gravy. (I like to add some chopped parsley to the gravy.)

Rasher Pudding

A savoury roly-poly of sorts, Rasher Pudding combines steamed suet dough with salty bacon and onion. There are recipes that date back to the eighteenth century and it became particularly popular amongst the traveller community in the UK, where tomato can often be found as an addition to the recipe. There are variations, such as the Sussex Bacon Pudding which often included sage, was wrapped in cloth and baked in a horseshoe shape.

Here, I have added the step of roasting the pudding after the steaming to achieve some crust for texture. I have also lightened the filling slightly with some toasted fennel seeds, lemon zest and pickled onions. For the shape of the pie, I thought something similar to a palmier when sliced would be attractive and still pay homage to the rolled appearance of the pudding.

Serves 6

800g suet pastry (see page 49)

1 egg yolk, strained and beaten with 1 teaspoon water, for egg washing

For the filling

500g Cumberland pork sausagemeat

200g pork mince

200g smoked bacon lardons

180g pulled ham hock meat

50g Beer-Pickled Onions (see page 255, or shop-bought pickled onions), finely sliced

Zest of 2 unwaxed lemons

5g sage leaves, finely chopped

3g fennel seeds, lightly toasted

Fine table salt

Method

Make the suet pastry no more than 2 hours before baking (as the raising agent in the self-raising flour needs to activate during steaming). Once made, flatten the suet pastry dough and chill in the fridge for at least 45 minutes (but no more than 2 hours) before using.

While the suet pastry is chilling, prepare the filling. In a large bowl, combine the sausagemeat, pork mince, lardons, ham hock, pickled onions, lemon zest, sage, 2g of the fennel seeds and 1 teaspoon of fine table salt, and mix together with your hands until well mixed.

Once the suet pastry has rested, roll it out on a lightly floured surface into a large rectangle. Trim that rectangle into two smaller rectangles, both roughly 22 × 42cm.

Divide the meat mixture equally into two. Roll out each half between two sheets of parchment paper so each is roughly 20 × 35cm.

Lightly brush the surface of each pastry rectangle with a little water and place the meat mixture centred along the bottom edge. Tightly roll up each rectangle into a long sausage, brushing a little more water over the exposed dough on the last part of the roll to seal. Turn the rolls so the seams are underneath. Close off the ends by squeezing the dough together, leaving about a 5cm thin flap. Trim off any excess with kitchen scissors and tuck neatly underneath.

Ingredients & method cont. overleaf

To serve

Spinach and Nutmeg Sauce (see page 249)

Place the two rolls side by side, so they are in contact, and wrap neatly in parchment paper. Finally, wrap that parcel loosely in foil so they are sealed in but not squeezed.

Preheat the oven to 165°C fan/185°C/gas mark 4.

Place a wire rack in a deep roasting tray, then sit the foil-wrapped parcel on top. Fill the tray with boiling water, stopping just below the level of the rack. Seal the entire tray with more foil.

Bake in the preheated oven for 3 hours. Carefully lift the parcel from the rack and transfer to a baking tray.

Turn up the oven temperature to 200°C fan/220°C/gas mark 7.

Remove the foil from the pudding and open up the parchment paper. Trim away the excess paper so only the paper just underneath the pudding is left. Lightly brush the exposed surfaces of the pastry with a little egg wash and scatter the remaining fennel seeds across the top.

Return the pudding to the preheated oven for 15 minutes to crisp the pastry. Allow the pudding to rest for 20 minutes before serving.

To serve, slice the pudding into thick slices. Spoon a small pool of the spinach and nutmeg sauce onto each plate and place a slice of the pudding on top, on its side to reveal the twin swirls of the Palmier shape.

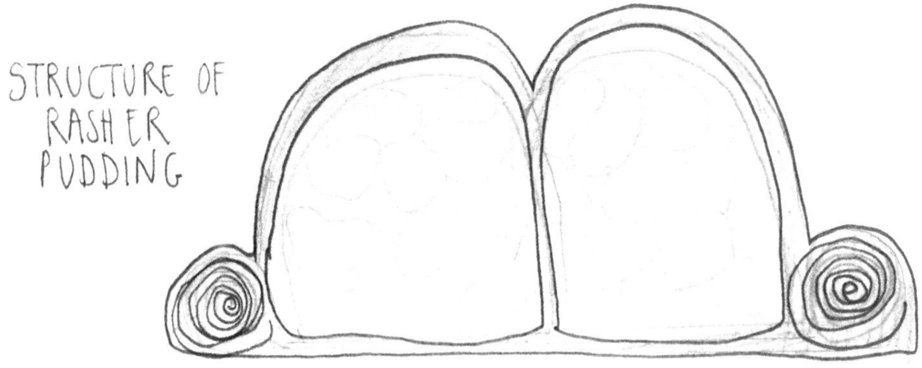

Lancashire Foots

Since the 1800s, these crescent-shaped pies were the food of field workers and miners in Lancashire, and so they were also known as Colliers' Foots (with a collier being a coal miner). The sharp, crumbly Lancashire cheese mixed with salty bacon makes for a really delicious filling. The horned pastry corners would have been a practical design feature, giving the workers something to hold the pie by, and then discard after eating, so their hands wouldn't dirty the rest of the pie. Locally, the plural of 'foot' remains as 'foots', and definitely not 'feet'.

My recipe is close to the original, with just the addition of a little mustard and the use of the Lancashire cheese as a sauce to give the filling a smoother texture. These handheld pies are incredible in the colder winter months.

Serves 4

1kg hot water crust pastry (see page 43)

1 egg yolk, strained and beaten with 1 teaspoon water, for egg washing

For the filling

150g smoked back bacon rashers

90g butter

60g plain flour

350ml semi-skimmed milk, warmed until hot

1 tablespoon vegetable oil

1 large brown onion, peeled and thinly sliced

350g cooked ham, cut into 1cm dice

130g Lancashire cheese, crumbled

1 tablespoon English mustard

Fine table salt and ground white pepper

Method

Preheat the oven to 180°C fan/200°C/gas mark 6 and line a baking tray with foil.

Spread the bacon rashers over the foil-lined tray and bake in the preheated oven for 14 minutes until crispy. Using a spatula or tongs, transfer the bacon to paper towels to remove any excess fat and allow to cool. Once cool, roughly chop the bacon.

In a large pan, melt 60g of the butter over a low heat. Add the flour and cook for a few minutes until just starting to brown, then add half of the hot milk and whisk until thickened and lump-free. Add the remaining milk and cook again whilst whisking until thickened and smooth. Turn off the heat and pour this white sauce into a bowl, cover with clingfilm and allow to cool to room temperature. Once cool, chill in the fridge for 30 minutes.

Meanwhile, heat the vegetable oil with the remaining 30g of butter in a small pan over a medium heat until bubbling. Add the onion with a pinch of salt and cook until any liquid released by the onion has evaporated. Turn down the heat to low and cook for a further 15 minutes until golden brown. Set aside to cool.

Fold the chopped bacon and cooked onion into the white sauce along with the ham, cheese and mustard, 1 teaspoon of fine table salt and ½ teaspoon of white pepper, mixing together until well combined.

Line a baking tray with parchment paper. On a lightly floured surface, roll out the dough to a square, 5mm thick. Slide the rolled-out pastry onto the lined tray and chill in the fridge for 30 minutes to rest.

Method cont. overleaf

Cut four 16cm circles from the pastry sheet. (You can squeeze any trimmings together, wrap them tightly in clingfilm and freeze to use another day.)

Divide the filling equally between the pastry circles, piling it up in an oval shape on one half of the disc and leaving a 1.5cm clear border of pastry. Lightly brush a little egg wash over the border on just one side of the circle, then carefully fold the clear side of the dough over to cover the filling, joining up with the egg-washed pastry. Press down the two layers of pastry along the curved edge to make sure the pie is well sealed, then really squeeze the two ends to make the dough thin and long enough to twist back around onto the pie to form the 'horns'. Lightly brush a thin coat of egg wash all over the pies, including under the horns to hold them in place. Chill in the fridge for 20 minutes.

Give the pies one final thin coat of egg wash, then score the tops of the pies a few times. (Scoring the pastry will prevent it from cracking as it expands in the oven.) Place the pies on the lined tray.

Preheat the oven to 200°C fan/220°C/gas mark 7.

Bake in the preheated oven for 30 minutes or until the pastry turns a deep caramel colour. Remove from the oven and allow to rest for 5 minutes before serving hot.

BEFORE I
address
ITS
BEGINNINGS,
WE NEED TO ASK
a
very
IMPORTANT
QUESTION:
IS THE
Cornish Pasty
A PIE
?

Cornish Pasty

This is one of the most important culinary creations in British food history. A dish with an enduring legacy and international influence, it has gone from a controversial origin story to accepted iconic status. It is a dish that evokes regional pride and deep emotion amongst many. However, before I address its beginnings, we need to ask a very important question: is the Cornish Pasty a pie?

At the 2016 British Pie Awards, a pasty created by Cumbrian butchers, A.F. Huddleston, was crowned Supreme Champion ahead of 815 other entries in a decision that sent shockwaves through the pie community. Matthew O'Callaghan, chairman of the British Pie Awards and Melton Mowbray Pork Pie Association, defended the decision at the time with a statement that read: 'The definition of a pie is a filling totally encased in pastry.' Others argued that this definition did not go quite far enough, asserting that a pie should have a bottom, sides and a top, whereas a pasty is simply a folded pastry. Regardless, the judges' decision stood firm and one thing that everyone agreed on was that the Beef Skirt and Vegetable Pasty was indeed superb – an exquisite example of British cookery. Because of that ruling in 2016, I decided that the Cornish Pasty does indeed have a place in this book. As much as that controversial viewpoint may upset some, I fear it will soon pale in comparison when we discuss the Cornish Pasty's history…

The first fact we need to establish is that the 'pasty' has been a documented part of British food history since Medieval times, often with a filling of venison and pork. Even recipes for pasties with a sweet fruit filling are abundant around this time. The Cornish Pasty is a relatively modern descendant of its Medieval ancestors, and a sub-section of the pasty family.

The widely accepted tale of the Cornish Pasty is that it was created in the nineteenth century by wives of Cornish tin miners, who wrapped a hearty meal of beef, potato and vegetables inside a robust pastry case. The crimped pastry edge could be discarded if it had been tainted by the dust of the work down the mine, once the unblemished interior had been eaten. However, in 2015 the historian Peter Brears put forward an essay in *Petits Propos Culinaires* (an international food history journal founded in 1979 by Alan Davidson, British Diplomat and food scholar) that called into question this origin story. Brears suggested that the Cornish Pasty as we know it, something that was cemented in form and structure and given full PDO (Protective Designation of Origin) status in 2011, was really created in London.

Brears posited that the Cornish Pasty's origins are likely a large, similar-shaped pasty filled with mainly vegetables and, on the odd occasion, some bacon trimmings. Beef would have been an unlikely filling given the cost implications. The theory advanced by Brears was supported by the historian Rachel Laudan who argued that, in the nineteenth century, fine white flour and fresh beef were 'beyond the means of miners driven by poverty to emigrate'. So, why London? Brears put forward that during the spread of National Cookery Schools and food education curriculum, a version of the Cornish Pasty was created in London to make use of meat trimmings in middle-class households, the pasty smaller than before, often only a few inches in length and filled with beef, potato and vegetables. He suggests that this was taught to thousands of housewives, school children and students and that this version of the Cornish Pasty became popular nationwide to the point where it was ultimately accepted by Cornwall as its official version.

Continued overleaf

It is important to point out that Brears' argument that this pasty was an 'English Pasty' rather than a 'Cornish Pasty' relies on the idea that the recipes taught in these classes did indeed break out into the commercial world rather than from Cornwall itself, but it does seem possible.

What is undeniable about the Cornish Pasty, whether it was an adopted recipe or something with unbreakable Cornish roots, is that it went on to have an incredible international influence, spreading out from the South West. As the industry faltered and Cornish miners struggled financially in the nineteenth century, many emigrated across the globe to look for work, and so too did the pasty. In researching, I have found recipes from Nigeria, South Africa, Australia, Mexico and America – all part of the Cornish mining diaspora of that time as the workers took their favoured meal with them globally. In Nigeria, the usual cut of beef chuck is replaced with the hump of the Zebu cattle, a highly marbled piece of meat. In Michigan, America, the pasty became part of the state's identity with bakeries from Hancock to Ironwood passionately competing with each other for the title of 'best pasty'. The Cornish mining community that moved to work in Real del Monte in the central Mexican state of Hidalgo established such a strong food tradition that there is now is an annual festival of *pastes* in October. Versions of the dish have adapted to suit the environment, ingredients and tastes of the Mexican state, with pasties including frijoles (beans), spices and herbs, and during the festival the flags of Britain and Cornwall fly proudly alongside Mexican flags.

Whether Brears' theory questions the true line of origin of Cornwall's precious pasty, it casts no shade over its later influence and importance for Britain's food history. I adore them. I feel they fall firmly into the 'hand pie' category… a transportable, convenient snack or lunch that is encased in a crust. My version here really doesn't stray too far from what is officially classified as a PDO Cornish Pasty, except that it is not made west of the river Tamar. I think shortcrust pastry is preferable to the optional puff pastry, as it is sturdier and better at locking in the moisture released by the beef and clotted cream. My preferred cut of beef is skirt (also known as bavette) as I think it behaves best in the cook given its fat content and tenderness; it is well worth seeking out some skirt from your butcher, but it is also readily available in supermarkets nowadays. Failing that, you could substitute the beef skirt for chuck. Dotting a knob of clotted cream onto the filling before sealing the pasty is a traditional way of adding richness. Lastly, do not be afraid to get some good colour and caramelisation on the crust of the pastry, which I think is important given the lack of it in the filling – the long cooking time will give you that.

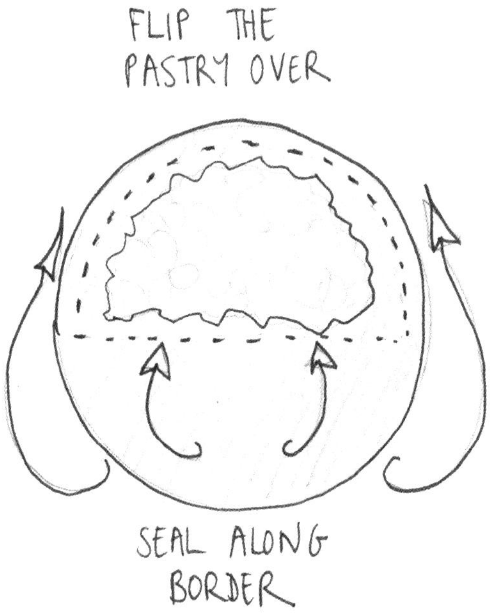

Serves 4

- 1kg shortcrust pastry (see page 32), or gluten-free shortcrust pastry (see page 36)
- 1 egg yolk, strained and beaten with 1 teaspoon water, for egg washing

For the filling

- 400g beef skirt (or chuck)
- 350g Maris Piper potatoes, peeled
- 250g swede, peeled
- 1 tablespoon plain flour
- 1 large Spanish onion, peeled and thinly sliced
- 4 tablespoons clotted cream
- Fine table salt, coarse sea salt flakes and ground white pepper

To serve

- Spiced Brown Ketchup (see page 250)

Method

Divide the dough into four equal balls. On a lightly floured surface, roll out each ball to a 5mm thick circle. Slide the rolled-out pastry onto a baking tray lined with parchment paper, with extra parchment paper between each pastry circle if stacking them, then place in the fridge to rest for at least 30 minutes.

To make the filling, cut the beef, potatoes and swede into 1.5cm dice – do not make the dice too big or the vegetables will not fully cook through.

Put the beef into a bowl and season well with 1 teaspoon of white pepper and a few big pinches of fine table salt. Dust the beef with the flour and then toss to coat.

Once well rested, lay the pastry discs on a lightly floured surface. Split the sliced onion, diced potatoes and diced swede equally between the discs, spooning them onto one half of each disc and leaving a clear border of 2–3cm around the edge. Sprinkle a little flaky sea salt over the vegetables. Top the vegetables with the diced beef. Finally, dot 1 tablespoon of clotted cream on each mound of filling.

Dab a little water onto the clear border of pastry on the half of the disc holding the filling. Fold over the other half of the pastry disc to cover the filling, aligning the edges. Press together the two layers of pastry around the curved edge to seal. You now have a D-shaped pasty. Lightly brush a thin coating of the egg wash over the exposed surface of the pasty. Next, twist a very simple crimp onto the curved edge, turning it in towards the centre with your thumb on each twist (see page 25).

Line a baking tray with parchment paper. Transfer the pasties to the lined tray and chill in the fridge for 20 minutes.

Preheat the oven to 200°C fan/220°C/gas mark 7.

Apply a final, thin coat of egg wash all over the exposed surface of the pasty, this time including the crimp. With the tip of a sharp knife, make a small cut right at the peak of the pasty to allow a little steam to escape.

Place the tray in the hot oven and bake the pasties for 20 minutes. Lower the oven temperature to 185°C fan/205°C/gas mark 6, turn the tray 180 degrees in the oven and cook the pasties for a further 40 minutes. Remove from the oven and allow the pasties to rest for 15 minutes as they will be piping hot inside.

Serve warm with a small bowl of spiced brown ketchup.

Welsh Corned Beef Pie

This pie was most likely a consequence of food rationing in Britain during the Second World War, when tinned corned beef fuelled the wartime nation as one of the only widely available forms of meat. Nonetheless, this pie ended up becoming beloved by many in Wales. In written recipes, it is often mentioned as something 'my grandma cooked' but with no real history passing before the mid-twentieth century, so this aligns with tinned corned beef coming over from the USA in those years.

It is, emphatically, one of my favourite pies in this book. When you take the time to get some deep caramelisation on the beef and potatoes, it really becomes a thing of beauty.

Serves 4

800g inverse puff pastry (see page 46, or shop-bought puff pastry)

1 egg yolk, strained and beaten with 1 teaspoon double cream

For the filling

500g new potatoes, halved if necessary

40ml vegetable oil, plus extra for greasing

1 large Spanish onion, peeled and thinly sliced

1 leek, trimmed of the top 3cm of green, washed and thinly sliced

3 thyme sprigs, leaves picked

20g butter

Method

Place the new potatoes in a large pan, cover with water and a good amount of salt. Bring to a gentle simmer and cook the potatoes until tender. Drain and set aside.

Heat half the oil in a large non-stick pan or frying pan over a medium heat. Add the onions and cook for a few minutes until soft. Add the leek and thyme leaves, then cook for a further few minutes. Transfer to a bowl and set aside.

In the same pan, heat the remaining oil with the butter over a medium heat. Once the butter has melted, add the cooked potatoes, gently breaking them up as they go into the pan. Cook for about 5–6 minutes or until the potatoes start taking on some colour and begin to sauté.

Crumble the corned beef into the pan with the potatoes. Sauté the beef and potatoes together, allowing the meat to caramelise, then stirring the mixture so the caramelisation is distributed throughout.

Return the onions, leeks and thyme to the pan. Stir in the mustard and Worcestershire sauce, then season with salt and pepper to taste. Cook for a few more minutes, letting the whole mixture take on some colour, then tip everything into a bowl. Allow to cool.

Ingredients & method cont. overleaf

2 × 340g tins corned beef
1 tablespoon wholegrain mustard
2 teaspoons Worcestershire sauce
Fine table and freshly ground black pepper

To serve

Steamed hispi cabbage
Beef and Stout Gravy (see page 246)

Equipment

20cm round pie tin

Grease the insides of the tin with a little vegetable oil, then line it with clingfilm. Tip the filling mixture into the lined tin and pack it down. Chill the tin in the freezer for 1 hour.

While the filling is in the freezer, prepare the pastry. Line a baking tray with parchment paper and divide the pastry dough into two equal pieces. On a lightly floured surface, roll out each piece to 5mm thick circle, 28cm in diameter. Slide the rolled-out pastry onto the lined tray and chill in the fridge for 30 minutes.

When the filling and pastry are both chilled, lay one pastry circle on a sheet of parchment paper and place the filling mixture in the centre. Lightly brush a thin coat of egg wash on the exposed border all the way round the filling. Drape the second pastry circle over the filling and gently push down to join the other disc, trying not to trap any air in the process. Trim the discs down so there is a 3cm border.

Lightly brush the exposed surface with a thin coat of egg wash. Crimp the 3cm border back onto the egg-washed pie top (see page 25). Chill in the fridge for 30 minutes.

Preheat the oven to 190°C fan/210°C/gas mark 6½.

Finally, give the pie one more thin coat of egg wash. Using a sharp knife, lightly score a design into the surface, being careful not to cut all the way through the dough. I decorated my pie with an abstract design of wavy lines that resembles tree bark or ocean waves. Make a small hole or cross in the centre of the pie lid for the steam to escape.

Bake in the preheated oven for 30 minutes or until the pastry turns a deep golden brown.

Serve slices of the pie with some steamed hispi cabbage and a jug of gravy.

Beef & Oyster Suet Pudding

This is a pie that has juggled its fillings over time. The first appearance of oysters in this beef pudding was in an 1845 recipe by Eliza Acton, whereas earlier recipes contained root vegetables alongside the meat. Steak made way for kidneys in Mrs Beeton's recipe in 1861. Perhaps more than any other, this pie has been affected by socio-economic factors. There was a period during the Victorian era, especially in London, when oysters would habitually be seen in pies. Oysters were a cheap source of protein as they grew in abundance around the coast… at least, until they didn't. The Industrial Revolution polluted British waters at a rapid rate during these years, which led to oysters suddenly becoming scarce and often dangerous to eat. Consequently, oysters made way for mushrooms, but again, it was short-lived as mushroom farming in Britain was inconsistent. For many years, the steak and kidney pudding reigned supreme – I remember it from school in the 1990s, although maybe I have always been trying to forget that trauma – until there was another shift.

In the early 2000s, I went to work at the The Ivy, the iconic London restaurant, where I learned from Mark Hix, the executive chef at that time. A trailblazing chef in many ways, just like Gary Rhodes, Mark turned his back on modern European cooking and brought focus to traditional historic British recipes through new eyes. Mark made dishes like Beef and Oyster Pudding fashionable again as the A-listers of the celebrity world sat down to eat them (usually next to a moaning Michael Winner, the controversial film director and restaurant critic).

Here, my recipe retains that striking flavour of the oysters paired with the beef, but replacing them with oyster sauce to avoid their slightly unusual texture. Then, as a nod to the fungi in those Victorian pies, I have included some sautéed oyster mushrooms. Unctuous nuggets of beef shin, which lend themselves to slow cooking, replace the beef chuck, which has a tendency to end up a little dry.

Serves 2–3

600g suet pastry (see page 49)

10g softened butter, for greasing

Method

First, making the filling. Pour the stock into a medium pan with a lid and bring to a simmer over a low heat. Add the beef shin, garlic, ginger, bay leaves and 1 teaspoon of fine table salt, place the lid on the pan and simmer over a low heat for 1½ hours. Using a slotted spoon, transfer the beef to a bowl, cover in clingfilm (to stop the meat drying out) and set aside. Remove and discard the bay leaves. Increase the heat to medium and reduce the remaining stock in the pan to 250ml. Add the oyster sauce to the stock, transfer to a jug and set aside.

Ingredients & method cont. overleaf

For the filling

600ml beef stock

350g beef shin, diced

1 large garlic clove, peeled and finely chopped

20g ginger, peeled and finely chopped

2 bay leaves

40ml oyster sauce

25g butter

35g plain flour

1 teaspoon picked thyme leaves

1 large Spanish onion, peeled and sliced into thin wedges

1 red onion, peeled and sliced into thin wedges

20ml vegetable oil

150g oyster mushrooms, torn in half

Fine table salt

To serve

Steamed tenderstem broccoli

Beef and Stout Gravy (see page 246)

Equipment

750ml (1-pint) ovenproof pudding basin

Wipe out the pan, then add the 25g of butter and melt over a low heat. Add the flour and cook, stirring continuously to stop it from burning, for about 3–4 minutes to make a roux. Gradually add in the reduced stock, no more than half at a time, whisking after each addition until smooth. Remove from the heat, then add the beef and thyme leaves to the pan with the sauce. Set aside to cool to room temperature.

Preheat the oven to 190°C fan/210°C/gas mark 6½. Line a baking tray with foil.

Scatter all the onion wedges over the lined tray. Drizzle the onions with the vegetable oil and toss to coat. Roast in the oven for 10 minutes, then add the mushrooms and continue cooking for a further 10 minutes. Add the roasted onions and mushrooms to the pan with the beef mixture and fold through to combine. Set aside to cool a little.

While the filling is cooling, make and chill the suet pastry dough (see page 49).

When ready to cook the pudding, grease the insides of the pudding basin with the butter. On a lightly floured surface, roll out three-quarters of the pastry dough to a large circle, 5mm thick, and use it to line the greased basin, gently pressing the dough against the sides, avoiding any creases and allowing any excess to hang over the rim. Roll out the remaining pastry dough into a smaller circle, also 5mm thick and at least as wide as the basin. Chill the lined basin and rolled out dough in the freezer for 10 minutes (or in the fridge for 15 minutes).

Preheat the oven to 160°C fan/180°C/gas mark 4.

Spoon the pie filling into the pastry-lined basin, filling it no more than three-quarters of the way to the top. (Once the pudding is sealed with the pastry lid, there needs to be at least a 1.5cm gap below the rim to allow for expansion during cooking.)

Trim the smaller pastry circle so it sits neatly inside the basin and lay it on the top of the pie filling. Wet the outer edge of the pastry lid with a little water. Trim the overhanging pastry back to about 2cm. Gently fold the overhanging pastry over from the sides onto the pie lid and lightly press it down to form a seal.

Cut a small circle of parchment paper to the same dimensions as the pudding basin, then sit it on top of the dough. Take a 25cm square of foil and fold a 2cm wide pleat down the centre of it. (The pleat will allow for some expansion during cooking if the dough rises above the rim of the pudding basin.) Loosely seal the basin with the foil and firmly tie a length of string around the rim to hold the foil in place.

Put the pudding basin into a deep roasting tray and pour in enough boiling water to come halfway up the sides of the basin, making sure the water does not reach the foil lid. Seal the whole tray with more foil.

Bake in the preheated oven for 2½ hours, checking the water level halfway through the cooking time and topping up if it's too low. Using a heatproof cloth, lift the pudding basin out of the roasting tray. Carefully remove the foil and paper, then leave to rest for 10 minutes.

When ready to serve, turn out the pudding: sit the basin on a damp dish towel and place a wide, deep-lipped bowl inverted over the top. With one hand pressed firmly on the base of the bowl and gripping the damp dish towel with your other hand, quickly flip over the basin so that the pudding now sits in the bowl. Remove the basin.

Serve the pudding immediately with some steamed tenderstem broccoli and a large jug of beef gravy to pour over the top at the table.

Peppered Steak Slice

The Peppered Steak Slice is a pie that dominates the hot snack industry in Britain and is eaten all across the nation. Probably the most contemporary recipe in this book, it does not have a deep history, but when it is made well, a Peppered Steak Slice is incredible. As with anything that is so simple, it can be easily levelled up by focusing on the quality of the ingredients and technique.

Instead of using regular black or white pepper here, I really encourage you to seek out the different types of peppercorns I recommend for this recipe. Kampot peppercorns from Cambodia have notes of red fruits and honey with less heat than many other varieties, whereas the Sarawak peppercorns from Malaysia are more floral and citrussy. Alongside brined green peppercorns, the Kampot and Sarawak peppers make an incredible, complex pepper sauce. After you've tried them, you may end up replacing your regular peppercorns for good.

The key to tender beef here is the flash frying; make sure your pan is super-hot and only brown the beef very briefly so it finishes cooking inside the pastry but the caramelised beef flavour is still there.

Serves 4

600g rough puff pastry (see page 44, or shop-bought puff pastry)

1 egg yolk, strained and beaten with 1 teaspoon water, for egg washing

For the filling

60ml vegetable oil

400g beef rump steak, fat and sinew removed, cut into 5mm thick strips

2 large brown onions, peeled and thinly sliced

50ml brandy

500ml beef stock

Ingredients & method cont. overleaf

Method

First, flash-fry the beef. (You may want to keep the kitchen door and windows open for this stage because of the smoke.) Place a heavy-based, wide saucepan over a high heat and get it very hot – if you drip a tiny splash of water into the pan, it should spin around in a ball shape rather than immediately turning into steam. Add half of the vegetable oil to the pan, then immediately put in half of the beef. Stirring continuously, very quickly brown the beef for no more than 1 minute. Using a spatula, transfer the beef to a plate and set aside. Repeat with the remaining oil and beef.

Once flash-fried, add a few pinches of fine table salt to the beef. (Salting the meat before frying will draw out moisture and make it harder to caramelise.)

Turn the heat down to low. Using the same pan, add the onions with a pinch of salt and stir them around until they release any water and start to soften. Turn up the heat a little and cook the onions while stirring occasionally until well caramelised and a toffee colour. If the onions are sticking to the base of the pan, add a little water every now and again.

- 250g Maris Piper potatoes, peeled and cut into 2cm dice
- 30g brined green peppercorns (drained weight), finely chopped
- 1 teaspoon freshly ground Kampot pepper
- ½ teaspoon freshly ground Sarawak pepper
- 4 thyme sprigs, leaves picked
- 1 heaped tablespoon cornflour
- Fine table salt

Pour the brandy into the onions and cook until reduced by half. Add any juices released by the flash-fried beef along with the beef stock and potatoes, then bring to a simmer and cook until the potatoes are just soft. Add in the peppercorns, ground pepper and thyme leaves and turn off the heat.

In a small bowl, make a slurry of the cornflour and a tablespoon of cold water. After a few minutes, stir the cornflour slurry into the onion and potato mixture. Bring everything back to a simmer, while stirring, for 1 minute, then turn off the heat. Set aside to cool to room temperature and then fold in the beef. Chill in the fridge.

Meanwhile, line a baking tray with parchment paper. On a lightly floured surface, roll out half of the pastry dough to a 30 × 25cm rectangle, 5mm thick. Roll out the other half of the dough in the same way. Slide the rolled-out pastry onto the lined tray and chill in the fridge for 30 minutes (or in the freezer for 15 minutes).

Preheat the oven to 200°C fan/220°C/gas mark 7.

Lay one of the pastry sheets in the centre of the parchment-lined baking tray. Spoon the beef filling onto the sheet, leaving a clear border at least 3cm wide along each edge. Lightly brush the border with a thin coat of egg wash. Take the other pastry sheet and drape it across the top of the filling, aligning the edges. Firmly press together the two layers of pastry all the way round the border to seal in the filling, starting from one end and working towards the other to avoid trapping any air. Lightly brush the surface of the pastry with a thin coat of egg wash, then pop it back in the fridge for 15 minutes (or in the freezer for 10 minutes).

Give the pastry a final thin coat of egg wash. Using the tip of a sharp knife, lightly score the pastry surface with your choice of decoration. I made lots of curved lines radiating from the centre of the rectangle towards the outer edge. When scoring, do not cut all the way through the dough. (It should feel as though the knife is just scratching the surface. Be at one with the knife.)

Bake in the preheated oven for 40 minutes, then serve immediately. The filling will be piping hot, but the pastry will be at its very best.

Mince & Cheese Pie

A British classic that made its way over to New Zealand in the 1900s, this pie fast became an absolute staple across that country, eventually taking over every cricket and rugby ground. Funnily enough, I think this pie is far more popular in New Zealand nowadays, although you can still find it at football grounds here in the UK. The pie culture in New Zealand (and Australia) mirrors so much of the pie culture in Britain. Whenever I visit, it brings me unbridled joy. I love how they take solace in pies while England are beating them at all sports.

This version of the classic Mince and Cheese Pie has some additional spices to bring a depth of flavour to the meat, very close to a chilli, but with a tang of acidity from the red wine vinegar to cut through the richness.

Serves 4–6

700g shortcrust pastry (see page 32, or shop-bought), or gluten-free shortcrust pastry (see page 36)

15g softened butter, for greasing

1 egg yolk, strained and beaten with 1 teaspoon water, for egg washing

For the filling

40ml vegetable oil

500g beef mince (20% fat)

1 large brown onion, peeled and finely chopped

2 green peppers, deseeded and cut into small dice

2 garlic cloves, peeled and minced

1 tablespoon chilli powder

1 teaspoon ground cumin

Method

Heat half of the vegetable oil in a wide-based pan over a high heat. Add the beef mince and cook until any liquid released has evaporated, breaking up any clumps with a wooden spoon. Turn down the heat to medium and continue to cook until the mince has started to brown, stirring occasionally. Drain the meat in a colander and set aside.

To the same pan, add the onion and peppers with the remaining oil and a good pinch of salt. Cook over a medium heat, stirring occasionally, until the onion is completely soft and starting to brown.

Turn down the heat to low, add the garlic, chilli powder, cumin, cayenne pepper and paprika, then cook for a further 2 minutes, stirring occasionally.

Stir in the tomato purée and cook for a minute. Add the chopped tomatoes, vinegar, Worcestershire sauce and sugar. Pour in the beef stock, return the cooked mince to the pan and bring up to a simmer. Cook until the liquid has reduced by about two-thirds and thickened, stirring every now and then to stop anything catching on the base of the pan. Taste to check the seasoning and add a little salt, if necessary. Turn off the heat and allow to cool for a few minutes.

Meanwhile, mix the cornflour with a tablespoon of cold water in a small bowl to make a slurry, then stir this into the mince mixture. Bring everything back up to a simmer and cook, stirring continuously, for 1 minute. Transfer the filling to a wide bowl and leave to cool to room temperature. Chill in the fridge.

Ingredients & method cont. overleaf

¼ teaspoon cayenne pepper
½ teaspoon smoked paprika
1 tablespoon tomato purée
400g tin chopped tomatoes
20ml red wine vinegar
1 tablespoon Worcestershire sauce
2 teaspoons muscovado sugar
500ml beef stock
1 heaped tablespoon cornflour
150g mature Cheddar, grated
100g mozzarella, grated
20g coriander leaves, roughly chopped
Fine table salt

To serve

Slow-roasted butternut squash with flaked almonds and chives
Tomato, Red Onion and Sherry Vinegar Salad (see page 260)

Equipment

Deep 20cm loose-bottomed fluted tart tin

Meanwhile, line a baking tray with parchment paper. On a lightly floured surface, roll out 300g of the pastry dough to a 24cm circle, 5mm thick. Roll out with the remaining 400g of dough to a 30cm circle, also 5mm thick. Slide the rolled-out dough onto the lined tray and chill in the fridge for 30 minutes.

Grease the tart tin with the butter. Line the greased tin with the larger pastry circle, nudging the dough all the way into the edges. There should be about 3cm of pastry overhanging the rim of the tin. Chill in the fridge for 20 minutes (or in the freezer for 10 minutes).

Fill the pastry case with the cooled filling. Combine the grated Cheddar and mozzarella, then fold through the chopped coriander. Spread the cheese mixture across the top of the filling, pressing it down so that when the cheese melts it doesn't leave a big gap between the lid of the pie and the mince filling.

Lightly brush the overhanging pastry with a little water. Lay the smaller pastry circle down over the filling, aligning the edges. Gently press the two layers of pastry together to form a lip that can be crimped (see page 25). Trim the overhanging pastry back to 3cm all the way round. Lightly brush the surface of the pastry with a thin coat of egg wash. Crimp the overhanging pastry down onto the lid, then pop in the fridge for 15 minutes.

Preheat the oven to 200°C fan/220°C/gas mark 7.

Give the pastry, including the crimp, a final thin coat of egg wash. Using a sharp knife, score the lid with any decoration you like without cutting all the way through the dough. I choose to score lots of fine diagonal lines to make an overall diamond pattern.

Bake in the preheated oven for 40 minutes. Remove the tin from the oven and sit it on a small upturned bowl to release the sides of the tin. Slide the pie from the base of the tin onto a serving plate, removing the base as you slide. If your tart tin does not have a loose bottom, serve the pie in the tin.

Serve with some slow-roasted butternut squash topped with toasted flaked almonds and chopped chives or a tomato, red onion and sherry vinegar salad.

Mince & Skirlie Pies

The Mince and Skirlie Pie is a relatively recent creation, born from two classic recipes both steeped in history and tradition: the Mince and Onion Pie and the Skirlie. A mix of oatmeal, onions and sometimes suet that is fried in a pan and often accompanies other dishes, Skirlie is so called due to the word 'skirl' which describes the sound it makes in the pan. Skirlie has been known as 'poor man's haggis'; to rectify this slur, I have included actual haggis in my recipe here. Recently Skirlie has been found on top of Mince Pies in Scotland – Bel's Butchers in Edzell makes a mean one – and I think it is a totally delicious combination.

Serves 4

500g beef dripping pastry (see page 48)

15g softened butter, for greasing

For the skirlie

40g beef dripping

30g butter

1 onion, peeled and finely diced

140g oatmeal

80g haggis

1 rosemary sprig, needles picked and finely chopped

Fine table salt and freshly ground black pepper

For the filling

50ml vegetable oil

250g beef mince (20% fat)

1 brown onion, peeled and finely diced

Ingredients & method cont. overleaf

Method

Line a baking sheet with parchment paper. Lightly grease the insides of the tart tins with the softened butter.

On a lightly floured surface, roll out the pastry dough to a 5mm thickness. Slide the rolled-out pastry onto the lined tray and chill in the fridge for 20 minutes (or in the freezer for 10 minutes).

Preheat the oven to 180°C fan/200°C/gas mark 6.

Cut out four 16cm circles from the pastry sheet and drop one into each of the greased tins. Lightly press the pastry against the sides of the tin, avoiding any creases or folds. Pop the tins back into the fridge for a further 15 minutes (or in the freezer for 10 minutes).

Prick the bottoms of the pastry cases all over with a fork. Cut four 16cm circles from parchment paper and use them to line the pastry cases, then fill each one to the rim with the baking beans.

Bake in the preheated oven for 20 minutes. Carefully remove the baking beans and the paper, turn down the oven temperature to 170°C fan/190°C/gas mark 5, then cook for a further 10 minutes. Remove from the oven and allow to cool.

To make the skirlie, melt the beef dripping and butter in a heavy-based pan over a medium-high heat. Add the onion with a good pinch of salt and cook until completely soft. Next, add the oatmeal and gently cook for 15 minutes until crispy. Crumble in the haggis and fold through the rosemary. Season with plenty of freshly ground black pepper. Set aside until needed.

1 large carrot, peeled and cut into 1cm dice

1 garlic clove, peeled and finely chopped

400g tin chopped tomatoes

500ml beef stock

2 rosemary sprigs, needles picked and finely chopped

1 heaped tablespoon cornflour

To serve

Buttermilk Mash (see page 264)

Beef and Stout Gravy (see page 246)

Equipment

Four 10cm non-stick, loose-bottomed, fluted tart tins

Ceramic baking beans

To make the filling, heat half of the vegetable oil in a wide-based pan over a high heat. Add the beef mince and cook until any liquid released has evaporated, breaking up any clumps with a wooden spoon. Continue to cook until the meat has started to brown, stirring occasionally. Drain the meat in a colander and set aside.

To the same pan, add the onion and carrot with the remaining oil and a good pinch of salt. Cook over a medium heat for about 8 minutes, stirring occasionally, until the onion is completely soft and starting to brown.

Turn down the heat to low, add the garlic and cook for a further 2 minutes, stirring occasionally.

Add the chopped tomatoes and beef stock. Return the cooked mince to the pan and turn up the heat to high. Cook until the liquid has almost evaporated, about 15 minutes, and the mince mixture is the consistency of a thick sauce. Turn off the heat.

Meanwhile, mix the cornflour with a tablespoon of cold water in a small bowl to make a slurry, then stir this into the mince mixture. Bring everything back up to a simmer and cook, stirring continuously, for 1 minute. As soon as the mixture has simmered for 1 minute, turn off the heat.

Preheat the oven to 190°C fan/210°C/gas mark 6½.

Fill the blind-baked pie cases three-quarters full with the mince filling. Divide the skirlie mixture equally between the pies, spooning it on top of the mince filling, ma. Place the tart tins back on the baking tray.

Bake in the preheated oven for 15 minutes or until the skirlie is well caramelised on top. Remove from the oven and pop the pies out of their tins by pushing up the loose bottom.

When ready to serve, spoon a good portion of buttermilk mash onto each plate and sit a pie on top. Place a jug of gravy on the table.

Tail Pie

This pie is based on a recipe known as Lambs' Tail Pie, which has more or less disappeared from sight in the UK but was popular during the nineteenth and twentieth centuries. There are strong roots for Lambs' Tail Pie in both the West Country and Kent, where sheep farming was prolific. Lambs' tails would be taken off the herd slightly later than normal, generally around six to nine months, so there was a bit more meat on them than usual. The tails would be skinned and boiled, then put into a shortcrust pastry case with parsley sauce. People would strip the meat off the bone as they ate the pie and the gelatine in the bones would thicken the sauce.

Most people will struggle to find lambs' tails nowadays, so this recipe uses oxtail and beef shin to provide a higher meat-to-bone ratio. It's equally delicious. I love the sticky meat you get from both of these cuts and would like to think that it keeps a little of the original pie's history alive. The black garlic adds a depth to the sauce that is really special, but if you cannot get hold of it, feel free to substitute regular garlic.

Serves 4–5

800g shortcrust pastry (see page 32, or shop-bought), or gluten-free shortcrust pastry (see page 36)

10g softened butter, for greasing

1 egg yolk, strained and beaten with 1 teaspoon water, for egg washing

For the filling

1kg oxtail

600g beef shin (off the bone)

Vegetable oil

1 small celeriac, peeled and cut into 2cm cubes

3 large carrots, peeled and cut into large wedges

Method

Preheat the oven to 200°C fan/220°C/gas mark 7.

Rub the oxtail and beef shin with 1 tablespoon of vegetable oil and place on a foil-lined roasting tray.

Coat the celeriac and carrots in another 1 tablespoon of vegetable oil and arrange over a separate foil-lined roasting tray.

Place the trays in the preheated oven and roast the meat and vegetables for 20 minutes.

Meanwhile, cut the onion in half through the root and then slice each half into six thick wedges, again through the root. Rub the onion wedges with a splash of vegetable oil.

After 20 minutes, remove the tray of roasted vegetables and set them aside to cool. Add the onion wedges to the tray with the meat and continue roasting for a further 10 minutes.

Once roasted, tip all of the meat and onion from the tray into an ovenproof casserole dish with a lid. Leave the celeriac and carrots out of the casserole dish for now – they will be added in later.

Lower the oven temperature to 160°C fan/180°C/gas mark 4.

Ingredients & method cont. overleaf

1 large brown onion, peeled but left whole

1 tablespoon tomato purée

440ml dark brown ale

1 litre beef stock

2 black garlic cloves, skins removed and flesh lightly crushed (or 1 garlic clove, finely chopped)

4 thyme sprigs

2 bay leaves

1 heaped tablespoon cornflour

Fine table salt

To serve

Steamed runner beans

Beef and Stout Gravy (see page 246)

Equipment

20cm square metal pastry ring, 4cm deep

In a medium pan, heat 1 tablespoon of vegetable oil over a low heat. Add the tomato purée and cook for 2 minutes. Pour in the ale, turn up the heat to medium and cook until reduced by half. Add the beef stock, black garlic, thyme sprigs, bay leaves and 10g of fine table salt, then bring to a simmer. Pour the stock mixture into the casserole dish over the meat and onions. Put the lid on the casserole dish, place it in the oven and cook for 3 hours.

After 3 hours, carefully remove the lid from the casserole dish and add the celeriac and carrots. Replace the lid and continue to cook in the oven for a further 30 minutes.

While the meat is cooking, take 300g of the pastry dough and roll it out to a 22cm square, 5mm thick. Roll out the rest of the dough to a slightly larger 30cm square, also 5mm thick. Lay the rolled-out dough on a baking tray lined with parchment paper, and chill in the fridge for at least 30 minutes.

Grease the inside of the pastry ring with the butter. Centre the pastry ring on the large square of chilled rolled-out dough. From the outer corners of the pastry ring, cut away a square of dough from each corner of the dough – this will help to fold the pastry into the square ring at the corners (see page 20).

Lift the pastry ring off the dough and sit it on a baking tray lined with parchment paper. Carefully lower the large square of dough directly onto the pastry ring – the cut-away corners should allow the pastry to fall neatly and evenly to the bottom. Gently press the dough into the sides of the pastry ring, making sure the dough settles right down into the creases. There should be about 2cm of pastry overhanging the lip of the ring all the way round the top – do not trim this collar. You can trim away any excess pastry from the corners where there is an overlap, but make sure there is enough dough to close the corners off properly. Neaten the sides, corners and collar and then pop the tray with the pastry ring into the fridge to chill until needed.

Once the meat is cooked, remove the casserole dish from the oven and turn off the heat. Remove the lid from the dish and allow everything to rest for 30 minutes.

Tip the contents of the casserole dish into a colander placed over a medium pan to drain the meat and vegetables. Remove and discard the thyme sprigs and bay leaves. Leave the contents of the colander to cool for 15 minutes.

Meanwhile, mix the cornflour in a small bowl with a tablespoon of cold water to make a slurry. Add this cornflour paste to the cooking liquid in the pan, place it over a medium heat and, whisking continuously, bring it up to a simmer and then cook for 1 minute to thicken the sauce.

Pick the meat from the oxtail and discard the bones. Add the pieces of oxtail to the pan along with all the remaining contents of the colander. Fold everything through the thickened sauce. Taste the sauce for seasoning and add a little salt if necessary. Leave the filling mixture to cool to room temperature, then place the pan in the fridge and chill for 30 minutes or until completely cold.

Remove the pastry-lined ring and rolled-out pastry lid from the fridge. Spoon the chilled pie filling into the pastry case and level the surface.

Lightly brush the collar of pastry overhanging the edges of the pastry case with a little water. Lay the smaller square pastry lid on top of the pie case. Using your fingers, firmly squeeze together the two layers of pastry where the lid meets the collar to seal the pie, thinning out the pastry in the process. Trim back the excess pastry with kitchen scissors to neaten and leave an overhang of 1.5cm. Lightly brush a 3cm border around the top of the outside edge with water. Fold the overhang over and down onto the brushed surface, pressing gently.

Flip the entire pie over onto the parchment paper so that the lid becomes the base of the pie. You now have a clean, smooth pastry surface as the top of the pie. Lightly brush the surface of the pie with a thin, even coating of egg wash. Chill the pie in the fridge for 15 minutes.

Meanwhile, preheat the oven to 200°C fan/220°C/gas mark 7.

Apply a second thin coat of egg wash to the pastry, then return the pie to the fridge for another 10 minutes. Using a small sharp knife, lightly score a decorative design into the surface of the pastry, taking care not to score right through. I like to start with a small square in the centre and then keep scoring larger concentric squares until I reach the outer edges.

Place the tray in the centre of the hor oven and bake the pie for 40 minutes.

Using the parchment paper to slide it over, carefully transfer the pie from the baking tray to a serving plate and remove the pastry ring. If the ring is being slightly stubborn, slide a small sharp knife around the edges.

Serve this pie with a generous jug of beef and stout gravy and some blanched runner beans tossed in lots of butter.

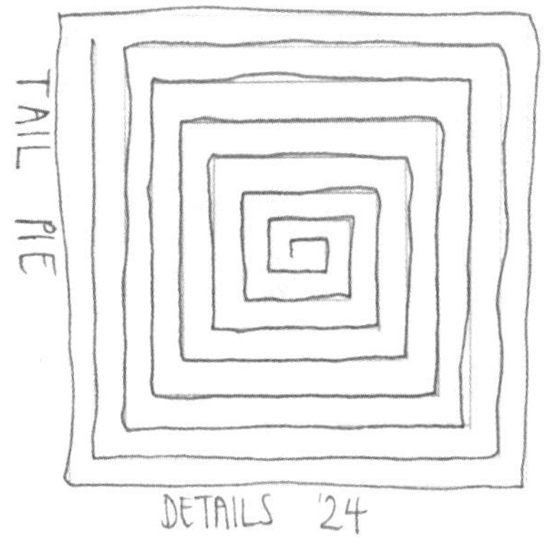

Teviotdale Pie

A suet crust pie with its origins in the Scottish Borders, specifically the Teviotdale valley where the town of Hawick lies, it reminds me of a cross between a cottage pie and mince and dumplings. The thick suet pastry crust would originally have been a way to bulk out the dish in face of a scarcity of meat. In my recipe, I have paid homage to that frugal aspect of the dish by adding Puy lentils into the beef filling, which my wife and I often do at home when we're trying to reduce our meat consumption. Adding cornflour into the mix stops the sauce from being fully absorbed by the suet pastry crust and keeps the filling moist.

Cornflour was patented in 1854 in Paisley, Scotland, by John Polson of Brown & Polson who produced it from maize. So that's another Scottish connection there too.

Serves 4–6

400g suet pastry (see page 49)

1 egg yolk, strained and beaten with 1 teaspoon water, for egg washing

For the filling

40ml vegetable oil

500g beef mince (10% fat)

1 large brown onion, peeled and thinly sliced

2 large carrots, peeled and cut into 1cm dice

1 tablespoon tomato purée

2 bay leaves

200ml red wine

10ml Worcestershire sauce

10ml sherry vinegar

250g cooked Puy lentils

500ml beef stock

2 rosemary sprigs, needles picked and finely chopped

Photographed overleaf

Method

Heat half the vegetable oil in a wide-based pan over a high heat for a few minutes. Add the beef mince and cook until any liquid released has evaporated, breaking up any clumps with a wooden spoon. Turn down the heat to medium and continue to cook until the mince has started to brown, stirring occasionally and adding a few pinches of salt during the process. Drain the meat in a colander and set aside.

To the same pan, add the onion and carrots with the remining oil and a few good pinches of salt. Cook over a medium heat, stirring occasionally, until the onion is completely soft and starting to brown.

Stir in the tomato purée, drop in the bay leaves and cook for a further few minutes. Pour in the red wine, Worcestershire sauce and sherry vinegar, then cook until the liquid has reduced by half.

Return the browned beef mince to the pan, add the lentils, beef stock, rosemary and ¼ teaspoon of white pepper, then bring up to a simmer. Cook until the liquid has reduced by at least half again and thickened, stirring every now and then to stop anything catching on the base of the pan. Turn off the heat and allow to cool for a few minutes.

Meanwhile, mix the cornflour with a tablespoon of cold water in a small bowl to make a slurry, then stir this into the mince mixture, making sure it is well combined. Bring everything back up to a simmer and cook, stirring continuously, for 1 minute. Taste to check the seasoning and add a little salt,

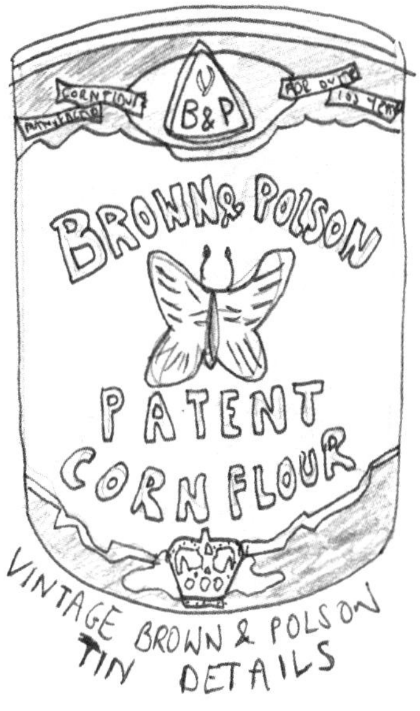

- 1 heaped tablespoon cornflour
- 4 thyme sprigs, leaves picked
- Fine table salt and ground white pepper

To serve

Roasted Cauliflower Cheese (see page 274)

Equipment

24cm oval or round ovenproof pie dish

if necessary. Turn off the heat and transfer the filling to the ovenproof dish, covering the base and levelling it with a spatula.

Preheat the oven to 190°C fan/210°C/gas mark 6½.

On a lightly floured surface, roll out the pastry dough to 1cm thickness. Cut out an oval or round to the same dimensions as the pie dish so that it fits inside the rim – err on the generous side with the cut so that the pastry doesn't shrink away too much from the sides. Lay the pastry across the top of the filling. Lightly brush the surface of the pastry with a thin coat of egg wash and sprinkle with the picked thyme leaves.

Bake in the preheated oven for 40 minutes. Do not worry if the sauce from the filling bubbles up the sides onto the pastry lid; that's the gold, embrace it.

Serve scoops of the pie with a whole roasted cauliflower cheese.

Scotch Pies

In her 1826 recipe book, *The Cook and Housewife's Manual*, Margaret Dods mentions the Scotch Pie as another name for the Brides' Pie. Mixing meats, fruits, spices and alcohol, a Brides' Pie was often a huge, elaborate, celebratory piece. What we now recognise as a Scotch Pie – a distant relative of the Brides' Pie – appears to have emerged during the early Victorian era, when Scottish pie makers would sell handheld Penny Mutton Pies that were relatively affordable for the masses. Far from being huge and elaborate, the Scotch Pie is allowed to be no wider than 5 inches (about 12cm), as enshrined in law; maybe the two were connected only through a filling of minced mutton. The differences between these two iterations of the same pie can perhaps be accounted for by a couple of hundred years of change; changes in taste, changes in fashion.

The Scotch Pie is made from a hot water pastry crust filled with minced lamb (or mutton), onions and spices (sometimes nutmeg, sometimes mace, sometimes both – although I prefer allspice as it has more complexity) and lots of white pepper. Very simple in appearance, the Scotch Pie is a small raised pie with a sunken lid. A practical design that means any juices boiling out of the meat filling are less likely to spill over the sides and be absorbed back into the pie as it cools down; the sunken lid is a pie maker's dream. My version of the Scotch Pie controversially introduces minced beef alongside lamb. Whilst I can hear the disapprobation of my late Scottish grandmother, I think it brings a delicious balance to the pie. I've also used beef dripping or tallow in the pastry, rather than lard, which again brings balance and ensures the lamb flavour isn't overly strong. I have stuck with the traditional shape of the Scotch Pie as, honestly, I think it's perfectly designed as it is. The shallow profile of the pie fits perfectly in the mouth, unlike a lot of handheld pies. Although do take just one bite at a time.

Serves 4

- 800g beef dripping pastry (see page 48)
- 10g softened butter, for greasing
- 1 egg yolk, strained and beaten with 1 teaspoon water, for egg washing

For the filling

- 20g beef tallow or dripping
- 250g beef mince (10% fat)

Ingredients & method cont. overleaf

Method

Weigh out 130g of the dough, roll it into a ball and then flatten it into a puck. Repeat this so you have four equal-sized pucks of dough. On a lightly floured surface, roll out each puck into a circle about 5mm thick.

Lightly grease the insides of the pie tins with the butter and line a baking tray with parchment paper.

Use the rolled-out dough to line the pie tins, making sure that the dough goes right into the edges of the base and all the way up the sides of the tin but being careful not to stretch the pastry or trap any air bubbles. Using a fork, prick the bottoms of the pie cases all over. Trim any excess dough from the tops of the tins to neaten. Place the tins in the fridge to chill the pastry for at least 1 hour.

250g lamb mince (10% fat)

1 large Spanish onion, peeled and finely chopped

400ml beef stock

2 teaspoons Worcestershire sauce

1 teaspoon ground allspice

1 teaspoon ground mace

1 heaped tablespoon cornflour

100g haggis, roughly grated

6 thyme sprigs, leaves picked and finely chopped

Fine table salt, sea salt flakes and ground white pepper

To serve

Spiced Brown Ketchup (see page 250)

Equipment

Four 10cm round non-stick pie tins (about 4cm deep)

Roll out the remaining dough into a square, 5mm thick, and slide it onto a parchment-lined baking tray. Place in the fridge to chill until needed.

In a wide pan, melt the beef tallow over a medium heat and warm for just 1 minute. Add the beef and lamb mince to the pan and sauté, stirring every few minutes, until the meat has browned. Strain off the excess fat, reserving a large tablespoon's worth, then set aside the meat in a bowl. Put the reserved fat back in the pan and add the chopped onion and 2 teaspoons of fine table salt. Sauté the onion over a medium heat for around 6–8 minutes until softened and lightly browned.

Return the meat to the pan along with the beef stock, Worcestershire sauce, ground spices and ½ teaspoon of ground white pepper. Simmer everything over a medium heat until the stock has reduced by three-quarters. Remove the pan from the heat.

Place the cornflour in a small bowl and stir in a tablespoon of cold water to make a slurry. Once the pie filling has stopped bubbling completely in the pan, quickly whisk in the cornflour slurry. Add the grated haggis to the pan, place it back over the heat and bring everything to a simmer, stirring continuously to prevent the mixture catching on the bottom of the pan. Finally, fold through the thyme leaves. Set aside the pie filling to cool.

Preheat the oven to 200°C fan/220°C/gas mark 7.

While the filling is cooling, take the sheet of rolled-out dough from the fridge and cut out four discs measuring 10cm in diameter for the pie lids. Using a very small pastry cutter or the wide end of a piping nozzle, punch a 1cm-wide hole out of the centre of each lid.

Once the filling is cool, take the pie cases from the fridge and evenly fill each one with a quarter of the mixture. Do not fill the pie cases up to the top – you want the filling to sit at least 1cm below the rim of the tin.

Lightly brush the outer edges of the pie lids with a little water, then place them with the wet edges facing downwards on top of the filled pie cases. Press the outer edges of each lid against the inside walls of the pie case to seal in the filling. Lightly brush the pie lids with a thin coat of the egg wash and sprinkle with a pinch of sea salt flakes.

Place the pie tins on a baking tray in the centre of the hot oven and bake for 30 minutes. Using a clean dish towel, carefully turn out each pie from its tin and put it back down onto the hot baking tray. Return the pies to the oven and cook for a further 5 minutes to ensure the bottoms of the pastry cases are crisp. Remove from the oven and allow the pies to cool on a wire rack for 10 minutes before serving with a big spoonful of fridge-cold spiced brown ketchup.

25

Forfar Bridies

The Bridie is thought to have originated in the early eighteenth century. There are two schools of thought on its beginnings, but in both, it is clear that the pie began in Forfar, just north of Dundee on Scotland's east coast. One story is that these pies were made popular by a baker called Maggie Bridie, who first created them for her wedding – the horseshoe shape being a symbol of good luck. Maggie Bridie went on to sell her pies at the Buttermarket in Forfar, where butter and other dairy products were sold; from there their popularity grew and spread across Scotland. Forfar Athletic Football Club has a Bridie as its mascot, which is amazing. Frankly, I am surprised there are not more pie-related mascots across Britain.

Traditionally, the Bridie houses a filling of minced beef inside shortcrust pastry. If it has one steam hole, that means the filling inside is plain mince. If it has two steam holes, that means there is the addition of onions. Mine have a few other additions, but instead of adding more steam holes – I would probably run out of pastry – I have made a small cross incision. I have also put my fillings inside a hot water crust pastry, which I think balances everything better.

Serves 4

800g hot water crust pastry (see page 43)

1 egg yolk, strained and beaten with 1 teaspoon water, for egg washing

For the filling

20ml vegetable oil

2 large brown onions, peeled and thinly sliced

500g beef mince (20% fat)

50g panko breadcrumbs, lightly crushed

1 teaspoon soft brown sugar

1 teaspoon Worcestershire sauce

1 teaspoon garlic granules

½ teaspoon smoked paprika

Method

Line a baking tray with parchment paper. Divide the pastry dough into four equal balls. On a lightly floured surface, roll out each ball to a 5mm thick oval, roughly 25cm long and 10cm wide across the centre. Slide the rolled-out pastry onto the lined tray and chill in the fridge for 30 minutes.

In a medium, heavy-based pan warm the oil over a medium heat. Add the onions with a pinch of salt, and cook, stirring continuously, until any water released by the onions has evaporated. Continue to cook the onions over a low heat until evenly browned, about 15–20 minutes. You are looking for the onions to turn a dark caramel colour. If the onions are sticking slightly to the pan, add a splash of water. Take the pan off the heat, spread the onions over a plate and leave to cool to room temperature.

In a bowl, combine the beef mince, panko breadcrumbs, sugar, Worcestershire sauce, garlic granules, paprika, 2 teaspoons of fine table salt and ½ teaspoon of ground black pepper. Do not overwork the mixture; it should be fairly loose in texture. Gently fold through the caramelised onions until evenly distributed. Divide the filling mixture equally and shape into four pucks.

Ingredients & method cont. overleaf

Fine table salt and freshly ground black pepper

To serve

Spiced Tomato Chutney (see page 254)

Lay the rolled-out pastry ovals on your work surface in a line. Arrange the pucks of filling mixture on one end of each pastry oval; if necessary, re-shape the filling so that there is a clear border of at least 1cm around the edges. Lightly brush the border around the filling with a thin coat of egg wash. Fold over the clear half of pastry to cover the filling, aligning the edges with the egg-washed border. (This gives the traditional horseshoe shape.) Gently press down on the egg-washed border to seal in the filling. Transfer to a baking tray lined with parchment paper and chill the Bridies in the fridge for 10 minutes.

Preheat the oven to 200°C/220°C/gas mark 7.

Using a fork, work all the way around the border of each Bridie, crimping it in place. Put the Bridies onto the lined tray. Lightly brush the exposed surface of each Bridie with a thin coat of egg wash. Finally, score a cross into the top of each Bridie to allow the steam to escape.

Bake the Bridies in the preheated oven for 35 minutes or until the pastry is a deep caramel colour. Remove from the oven and allow to cool for 10 minutes.

Serve while still warm or at room temperature with a spoonful of tomato chutney and a strong cuppa.

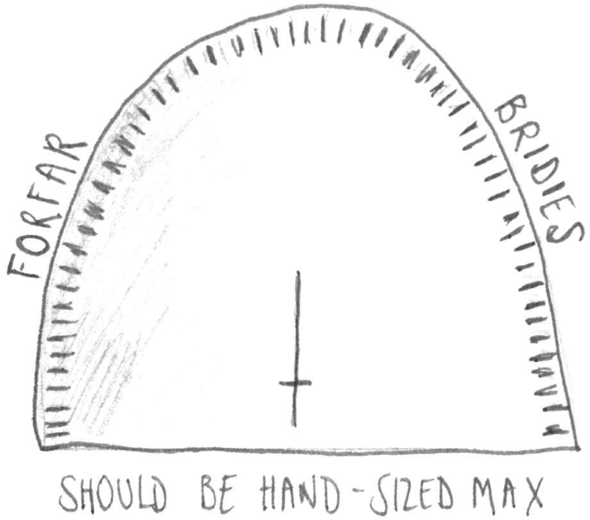

Shepherd's Pie

Probably the pie that I remember eating the most during my childhood; whether at school or at home cooked by my mum, Shepherd's Pie dominated the dining tables of my youth. Looking back at early mentions, it is clear that it was a dish designed to use up leftovers. The first recorded recipe was written in *The Practice of Cookery and Pastry* in 1849, in Scotland; it did not specify exactly what meat to use other than 'sliced', so probably was devised as a good way to use up cold, cooked meats. Over time, the Scottish version of this pie varied to include a thin layer of crisp pastry, but I'm going with my favourite mash topping instead. The Irish stuck to minced lamb and mashed potato, whilst in England its popularity waned due to the dominance of the Cottage Pie as a consequence of cattle farming.

The pie that I knew and loved was always simple, the flavour coming from the browning of the lamb mince, so I think that the Scottish layer of pastry is not vital to the dish. Here, I have added a little black garlic for some depth of flavour, but feel free to swap that for regular garlic if you cannot find the black variety. For me, the sweet potato blended into the mash topping complements the lamb flavour well, almost like it should have always been there.

Serves 4–6

600g sweet potatoes

1kg Maris Piper potatoes, peeled and cut in quarters

30g butter

1 egg yolk

Fine table salt

For the filling

30ml vegetable oil

1 large brown onion, peeled and finely diced

2 large carrots, peeled and cut into 1cm dice

4 celery sticks, peeled and cut into 1cm dice

1kg lamb mince (10% fat)

Ingredients & method cont. overleaf

Method

Preheat the oven to 180°C fan/200°C/gas mark 6.

Prick the sweet potatoes all over with a fork and put them onto a foil-lined roasting tray. Bake in the preheated oven for 40 minutes or until they pierce easily with the tip of a knife. Allow to cool for 5 minutes, then cut in half, scoop out all the flesh and discard the skins.

While the sweet potatoes are baking, rinse the quartered potatoes under cold water for a few minutes to remove as much starch as possible. Place the potatoes in a medium pan, cover with fresh water, bring to a simmer and cook until just soft throughout, around 15 minutes. Drain the potatoes in a colander and allow them to steam for 5 minutes.

Pass the potatoes through a ricer, then mix with the sweet potatoes, fold in the butter and season with fine table salt to taste. (If you do not have a potato ricer, crush them really well with a potato masher before adding the butter and salt.) Set aside to cool.

Heat the vegetable oil in a wide-based pan over a medium heat for a few minutes. Add the onion, carrots and celery with a pinch of salt and cook,

2 black garlic cloves, peeled and crushed (or 1 garlic clove, finely chopped)

1 litre lamb stock

20ml red wine vinegar

20ml Worcestershire sauce

4 rosemary sprigs, needles picked and finely chopped

1 heaped tablespoon cornflour

To serve

Lancashire Peas (see page 270)

Equipment

Potato ricer (optional)

Large oval ovenproof dish (roughly 30cm in length)

Piping bag (optional)

stirring occasionally, until the onion is soft, around 5 minutes. Transfer the vegetables to a plate and set aside.

To the same pan, add the lamb mince with 2 teaspoons of fine table salt and cook until any liquid released has evaporated, breaking up any clumps with a wooden spoon. Continue to cook until the mince has started to brown.

Turn down the heat to low, stir the black garlic (or regular garlic) well through the mince and cook for a few minutes without browning. Add the lamb stock, red wine vinegar and Worcestershire sauce, return the cooked vegetables to the pan and bring everything up to a simmer. Cook until almost all the liquid has evaporated. Fold through the chopped rosemary and turn off the heat.

Mix the cornflour with a tablespoon of cold water in a small bowl to make a slurry, then stir this into the mince mixture, making sure it is well combined. Place the pan back on the heat and bring everything up to simmer and cook, stirring continuously, for 2 minutes. Taste to check the seasoning and add a little salt, if necessary. Turn off the heat and transfer the filling to the ovenproof dish, covering the base and levelling it with a spatula.

Preheat the oven to 180°C fan/200°C/gas mark 6.

Beat the egg yolk into the mashed potato mixture. Spoon the mash into a large piping bag and pipe the potato topping across the surface of the lamb mince filling in the dish. You can do this in any way you like; I pipe lots of rows made up of short lines on the slight diagonal until the entire surface is covered. Alternatively, spoon the potato topping evenly over the filling, then ruffle the mash for added texture.

Bake in the preheated oven for 35 minutes or until the potato topping is nicely browned and crispy and the lamb mixture has bubbled up the sides of the dish.

Serve immediately, spooning portions of the pie onto each plate, with some Lancashire peas on the side.

Katt Pies

The origins of this pie can be traced back to Pembrokeshire in south west Wales, where it has been eaten on 12th November at the Templeton Fair for over 200 years. Traditionally the filling was lamb with a few spices and currants; it would have been delicious but relatively dense. Here I have lightened it with minced lamb in a tomato base and replaced the currants with apricots, which I feel are a better fit. The addition of tomato into the recipe also stops it from becoming dry.

There have never been, as far as I have ascertained in my research, any cats involved or harmed in the cooking of this recipe. As Bobby Freeman mentions in her book, *Welsh Country Puddings and Pies*, there is actually no letter 'K' in the Welsh alphabet, which further adds to the mystery. The more likely explanation is that the pie was named after the butcher who first created it.

Makes 8 small pies

800g hot water crust pastry (see page 43)

30g softened butter, for greasing

5g fine semolina, for dusting

1 egg yolk, strained and beaten with 1 teaspoon water, for egg washing

2 rosemary sprigs, needles picked and finely chopped

For the filling

1 tablespoon vegetable oil

250g lamb mince (10% fat)

50g butter

1 brown onion, peeled and finely chopped

1 garlic clove, peeled and finely chopped

300ml lamb stock

Ingredients & method cont. overleaf

Method

Heat the vegetable oil in a wide-based pan over a medium heat for a few minutes. Add the lamb mince and cook, breaking up any clumps with a wooden spoon, until the meat is lightly browned. Drain the meat in a colander and set aside.

In the same pan, melt the 50g of butter over a medium heat. Add the onion and cook, stirring occasionally, for 10 minutes until completely soft and starting to brown. Add the garlic and cook for another minute.

Return the lamb mince to the pan and add the stock, tomatoes, paprika and cinnamon stick, and season with 1 tablespoon of fine table salt and 1 teaspoon of pepper. Cook until the liquid has reduced by half. Turn off the heat and remove the cinnamon stick.

Mix the cornflour with a tablespoon of cold water in a small bowl to make a slurry, then stir this into the mince mixture. Bring everything back up to a simmer over a medium heat and cook, stirring continuously, for 1 minute or until thickened. Fold through the apricots and mint leaves. Set aside to cool.

On a lightly floured surface, roll out 500g of the pastry dough to 5mm thickness. Using a 10cm round pastry cutter, cut out eight circles from the dough and set aside. Roll the remaining pastry dough in the same way, then cut out 8cm discs, re-rolling the trimmings to get eight in total. Punch out a 1cm hole from the centre of each small disc. (If you do not have a pastry cutter small enough, you could use the wide end of a piping nozzle or even a pen lid, providing it is clean.)

2 medium tomatoes, roughly chopped
1 teaspoon smoked paprika
1 cinnamon stick
1 heaped tablespoon cornflour
100g dried apricots, roughly chopped
Few fresh mint sprigs, leaves picked and roughly chopped
Fine table salt and freshly ground black pepper

To serve

Buttermilk Mash (see page 264)
Mint and Caper Sauce (see page 247)

Equipment

10cm, 8cm and 1cm round pastry cutters
12-hole non-stick muffin tin

Grease eight of the holes of the muffin tin with the 30g of butter and dust with half of the semolina. Line the holes with the larger pastry discs, pressing the dough right into the edges of each base and all the way up the sides but being careful not to stretch the pastry or trap any air bubbles.

Once the filling is cool, evenly fill each of the pastry cases with the lamb mixture. Do not fill the pie cases up to the top – stop three-quarters of the way up the sides.

Lightly brush the outer edges of the pie lids with a little water, then place them with the wet edges facing downwards on top of the filled pie cases. Press the outer edges of each lid against the inside walls of the pie case to seal in the filling. Lightly brush the pie lids with a thin coat of the egg wash and dust the tops with the remaining semolina. If you like, you can pinch in the sides of the pies to mould the pies into an X-shape. Scatter the finely chopped rosemary over the tops of the pies. Chill in the fridge for 30 minutes.

Preheat oven to 200°C fan/220°C/gas mark 7.

Place the muffin tin directly on the rack in the centre of the preheated oven and bake for 35 minutes. Remove from the oven and leave the pies to cool for 10 minutes.

Serve the pies hot either as a snack on their own or as a meal with buttermilk mash and mint and caper sauce heaped over the top.

Welsh Oggie

The Oggie has strong links to Cornwall and its not too distant or dissimilar to its cousin, the pasty. However, the Oggie has also found its way deep into the heart of Welsh culture; you will find them at festivals and celebrations all over the country. The Oxford English Dictionary describes 'oggie' as a likely abbreviation of the Cornish word 'hoggan', which means pasty. Like pasties, Oggies were eaten for lunch by miners working in the coal industry; substantial and nutritious, they were designed to keep going those working as hard physical labourers.

My take on the Welsh Oggie uses lamb neck, which lends itself well to slow cooking, prior to being encased in a hot water pastry crust. I think it creates a delicious pie. Oggies are usually large, often larger than a single portion, so here I have made one giant Oggie to serve everyone, rather than fiddling with lots of individual pies. It makes the whole dish more celebratory, and is much more fun.

Serves 4

500g hot water pastry (see page 43)

1 egg yolk, strained and beaten with 1 teaspoon water, for egg washing

For the filling

400g diced lamb neck

40ml vegetable oil

3 Spanish onions, peeled and thinly sliced

1 litre lamb stock

2 garlic cloves, peeled and bashed

3 rosemary sprigs, needles picked and finely chopped, stalks retained

3 mint sprigs, leaves picked and torn, stalks retained

Ingredients & method cont. overleaf

Method

Preheat the oven to 200°C fan/220°C/gas mark 7.

To make the filling, evenly season the diced lamb with 2 teaspoons of fine table salt and a few twists of black pepper, then drizzle over half of the oil and rub it into the meat. Spread the lamb over a deep roasting tray and roast in the preheated oven for 25 minutes.

Meanwhile, warm the remaining oil in a wide pan over a medium heat. Add the sliced onions along with 1 teaspoon of fine table salt and, stirring occasionally, cook for 15–20 minutes or until the onions are caramelised and well browned. If the onions are catching on the bottom of the pan, add a splash of water.

Pour the lamb stock to the pan, add the bashed garlic and bring everything to a simmer. Tie the rosemary and mint stalks together with string and drop them into the pan.

Once the lamb has roasted, lower the oven temperature to 165°C fan/185°C/gas mark 4½.

Pour the stock mixture into the roasting tray over the lamb. Cover the tray with foil and cook in the oven for 2½ hours.

Remove the tray from the oven and carefully peel back the foil. Strain off the stock into a separate pan, discarding the garlic cloves and rosemary and mint stalks, but setting aside the lamb and onions.

400g Maris Piper potatoes, peeled and cut into 2cm dice

3 leeks, trimmed of the top 3cm of green, rest washed and thinly sliced

Fine table salt and freshly ground black pepper

To serve

Green Herb Sauce (see page 248)

Bring the stock to a simmer over a medium heat, skimming off as much of the fat that rises to the surface as possible. Add the diced potatoes to the pan and cook in the stock for about 10 minutes or until just soft. Using a slotted spoon, remove the potatoes and set aside to cool.

Add the leeks to the pan and cook for 1 minute, then remove and set aside with the potatoes.

Finally, reduce the remaining stock over a low heat until it is thick enough to coat the back of a spoon.

Return the lamb and onions, potatoes and leeks to the pan with the reduced stock, stirring well so that all the ingredients are well coated. Fold in the chopped rosemary and torn mint, then check the seasoning and adjust as necessary. Set aside the filling to cool, then chill in the fridge.

Line a large baking tray with parchment paper. On a lightly floured surface, roll out the pastry dough to large circle, 5mm thick. Trim the pastry circle to 30cm in diameter, retaining any trimmings for decoration, then slide it onto the lined baking tray and chill in the fridge for 10 minutes.

When both the pastry and filling are chilled, spoon the filling onto one half of the pastry disc, leaving a 3cm clear border around the edge. Lightly brush the pastry border around the filling with a thin coat of the egg wash. Fold over the clear half of pastry to cover the filling, aligning the edges with the egg-washed border and creating a half-moon shape. Gently press the curved edges together to seal in the filling and thin out the double layer of pastry.

Leaving the Oggie on the lined baking tray, lightly brush the exposed surface of the pastry with a thin coat of the egg wash and then crimp the pastry border along the curved edge (see page 25). Chill in the fridge for 10 minutes.

Preheat the oven to 190°C fan/210°C/gas mark 6½.

Now, add any decoration to the Oggie using the reserved pastry trimmings. I added nine small half-moon shapes, each with a lightly scored curved edge to echo the overall shape of the Oggie, placed randomly over the surface of the pie. Lightly brush the Oggie with the egg wash for a final time, then score a cross in the top to allow the steam to escape.

Bake in the preheated oven for 35 minutes or until the pastry is golden brown.

Serve while still warm with the green herb sauce and some steamed green beans.

Buckinghamshire Rabbit Pie

This pie is likely a twentieth-century invention, as many recipes for it feature macaroni pasta, which only really became popular in the UK during the very late nineteenth century. This pie has been eaten in and around Buckinghamshire since its conception, which is likely where the addition of the pasta occurred. I much prefer the earlier recipes that do not include the macaroni pasta and cream additions; it leaves you with a lighter pie and one that focuses the attention more on the delicate rabbit flavour.

Sometimes the rabbit appears as a raw meat, stripped from the bones and mixed with pork, before baking in a double puff pastry case. Other times the rabbit has been pre-stewed for a few hours, which I think would leave the meat a little dry. For this version, I have gone with a raw mixture for the pie filling as it allows you to create a really beautifully shaped pie. Ask your butcher to take all the meat off the rabbit for you and get them to cut the loins into 2cm dice. Keep the loins separate from all the other rabbit meat, which will be minced later.

Serves 4–5

700g inverse puff pastry (see page 46, or shop-bought puff pastry)

10ml vegetable oil, for greasing

1 egg yolk, strained and beaten with 1 teaspoon water, for egg washing

For the filling

1 whole rabbit, meat trimmed from the bones (ask your butcher)

500g pork mince (20% fat)

60g smoked pancetta, diced

100g prunes, roughly chopped

Method

Put all the rabbit meat, except the loins, in a food processor and pulse until roughly minced. (If you don't have a food processor, finely chop the meat with a sharp knife.) Combine the diced loin, minced rabbit and pork mince in a large bowl. Season with 2 teaspoons of fine table salt and ½ teaspoon of white pepper. Fold in the pancetta, prunes, tarragon and crushed panko breadcrumbs, mixing everything well together.

Grease the insides of the tin with the oil. Tear off a large sheet of clingfilm and use it to line the tin. (The oil will help to get the clingfilm down into the edges.)

Spoon the pie filling into the clingfilm-lined tin, packing it down to make sure it goes right down to the edges and with no gaps or air pockets. Pop the tin into the freezer for 30 minutes.

Meanwhile, line a baking tray with parchment paper. On a lightly floured surface, roll out one-third of the pastry to a 24cm circle, 5mm thick. Repeat with the remaining pastry to make a larger circle, about 30cm, also 5mm thick. Slide the rolled-out pastry onto the lined tray and chill in the fridge for 25 minutes.

Photographed overleaf

6 tarragon sprigs, leaves picked and roughly chopped
50g panko breadcrumbs, lightly crushed
Fine table salt and ground white pepper

To serve

Roasted Cauliflower Cheese (see page 274)
Steamed spring greens

Equipment

20cm springform cake tin

Once both the rolled-out pastry and pie filling are chilled, lay the smaller pastry circle on a sheet of parchment paper. Unclip the sides of the springform cake tin and gently lift it off the pie filling. Using the clingfilm, carefully transfer the pie filling onto the centre of the pastry circle, leaving an even, clear border all the way around. Remove the clingfilm.

Lightly brush the clear border of dough around the pie filling with a thin coat of egg wash. Lay the larger pastry circle directly across the pie filling and gently press the dough against the top and sides, trying not to trap any air bubbles while you do so. Seal the two pastry layers by pressing down onto the egg-washed border.

Lightly brush all the exposed surfaces with a thin coat of egg wash. Crimp the edges of the sealed border up and onto the sides of the pie (see page 25). Chill in the fridge for 20 minutes.

Preheat the oven to 200°C fan/220°C/gas mark 7.

Give the entire pie one more thin coat of egg wash, including the crimp, and then lightly score the surface of the pie with any decoration you like. I chose to decorate my pie with an intricate repeating pattern of interlocking fan or shell shapes.

Bake in the oven for 45 minutes or until it reaches an internal temperature of 65°C on a digital probe thermometer, turning the pie 180 degrees in the oven halfway through the cooking time. Remove from the oven and allow to rest for 10 minutes before serving.

Slice the pie into large wedges and serve alongside roasted cauliflower cheese and some generously buttered and peppered steamed springs greens.

SWEET PIES

Apple Pie

Recipes for apple pies are found as far back as the fourteenth century in Britain, with one even written by Chaucer; however, these were almost all savoury pies with some spicing. It was not until the seventeenth and eighteenth centuries, when sugar was more readily available, that apple pies began to resemble the sweet dish that we know and love today. One of the reasons that the Apple Pie has endured for so long throughout Britain's history without ever disappearing must be down to our excellent native apple varieties. If there is a better apple for a pie than a Bramley, I am yet to find it. Its tartness is perfect for this dish.

Here, my recipe pays homage to the apple and Cheddar pies of the 1800s, a popular pairing in nineteenth-century Britain when cheese would frequently top fruit pies. But instead of adding slices of cheese, I have incorporated grated mature Cheddar into the pastry to give a tangy, savoury balance to the tart, sweet filling. The addition of Granny Smith and Cox's apples to sit alongside the mighty Bramley brings some extra texture to the pie filling (especially when thickly sliced) and also reduces the amount of sugar you need to add as both are naturally sweet.

Serves 4–6

600g Cheddar shortcrust pastry (see page 34), or gluten-free shortcrust pastry (see pages 36)

10g softened butter, for greasing

10g caster sugar, for dusting

1 egg yolk, strained and beaten with 1 teaspoon water, for egg washing

For the filling

100g butter

Zest and juice of 1 lemon

3 Bramley apples, peeled, cored and roughly diced

110g light brown soft sugar

30ml apple cider vinegar

Method

On a lightly floured surface, roll out two-thirds of the pastry dough to a large circle, about 5mm thick. Slide the rolled-out pastry onto a parchment-lined baking tray and chill in the fridge for 20 minutes. Repeat for the remaining dough, rolling it out into a slightly smaller circle but also about 5mm thick; chill this too.

Meanwhile, make the filling. Put 50g of the butter in a wide pan and cook over a medium heat until it starts brown and smell nutty. Immediately remove from the heat, then pour in the lemon juice to stop it cooking. Add the remaining 50g of butter and melt over a low heat, then stir in the diced Bramley apples, lemon zest, sugar, vinegar, ground cinnamon and 50ml of water. Mix everything well, then cover the pan with a lid and cook for 5 minutes, stirring occasionally. Once the Bramley apples have properly broken down, fold in the sliced Granny Smith and Cox's apples and thyme leaves. Set aside to cool.

Grease the insides of the pie tin with the 10g of softened butter and then dust it with a few pinches of the caster sugar. Line the tin with the larger disc of pastry. Press the dough firmly against the sides of the tin and into the edges, making sure it is in contact with the tin throughout. Allow the excess pastry to come up and over the top edge, overhanging by at least 3cm. Chill the pastry case in the fridge for 15 minutes.

Ingredients & method cont. overleaf

- ½ teaspoon ground cinnamon
- 2 Granny Smith apples, peeled, cored and thickly sliced
- 2 Cox's apples, peeled, cored and thickly sliced
- 2 thyme sprigs, leaves picked

To serve

Proper Custard (see page 277) or Calvados Cream (see page 275)

Equipment

20cm round springform tin or pie tin

Using a fork, prick the bottom of the pastry case all over and then fill it with the cooled apple filling, stopping a few centimetres below the top edge.

Rather than adding any decoration made from offcuts of pastry to the pie lid, I punched out a series of different size holes randomly over the smaller disc of pastry using a selection of pastry cutters. Once in place, the apple filling is revealed beneath the lid.

Lightly brush the overhanging pastry border with the egg wash. Gently lay the smaller pastry disc over the top of the fruit filling, matching the edges up to the egg-washed overhanging border. Gently pinch the two layers of dough together all the way round the edge. If necessary, using a pair of kitchen scissors, trim the overhang back to a neat 3cm border.

Lightly brush the surface of the pastry with the egg wash. Crimp the 3cm border up and onto the lid of the pie to make a decorative edge (see page 25). If you prefer to add some extra decoration to the pie lid, instead of punching out the holes, do it now. Dust the pastry lid with the remaining caster sugar. Chill the pie in the fridge for 20 minutes.

Preheat the oven to 185°C fan/205°C/gas mark 6½.

If you have punched out holes from the lid, there is no need to make a steam hole. Otherwise, cut a cross into the centre of the pie lid using a small, sharp knife, making each cut about 2cm long. Gently tease the corners of the cross open to create an air vent to allow any steam to escape the pie.

Place the tin in the preheated oven and bake the pie for 40 minutes or until the pastry is deep golden brown. Remove the pie from the oven and allow to rest for 10 minutes before slicing.

Serve slices of the pie with a jug of custard or some calvados cream, if you are feeling particularly posh.

Sussex Pond Pudding

This is a recipe that will forever remind me of the iconic British chef, Mark Hix. It was while I was in my twenties that I came across his recipe for Sussex Pond Pudding, first published in his 2003 cookbook, *British*. A steamed suet pudding that unusually houses a whole lemon inside, as Hix writes that the fruit 'serves two purposes: one to hold the pudding up and secondly to permeate the rich buttery sauce with a delicate lemony flavour as it cooks'. It is this sauce that creates the pond in which the pudding sits once it is turned out onto a plate. By all accounts, the inclusion of a whole lemon inside the pudding is a relatively modern approach, a trend likely started by cookery writer Jane Grigson through her recipe book, *English Food*, in 1974. The first written recipe for this pudding, however, appears to be in a 1672 book, *The Queen-Like Closet*, by Hannah Woolley. The traditional Sussex Pond Pudding sees fruits, butter and sugar encased in a suet crust, then steamed until the fruits soften. Very early recipes would not have included the lemon; instead, a great lump of butter would have taken its place. The fat would melt during cooking, but its volume was too large to be fully absorbed by the sponge and so it would leak out to create the 'pond' of sauce.

My main adaptation to this classic recipe is swapping the usually discarded whole lemon for cooked citrus fruits. During recipe testing, I found that it took a very, very long time to steam a suet pudding to the point that the whole lemon buried within was fully edible, so I have returned to the more traditional sliced citrus fruits. I love the idea of the whole lemon and how it permeates the pudding, but it does mean that such a large percentage of the finished dish is inedible. It made sense to tackle that. By blanching the citrus fruits, their bitterness is removed and they become soft enough to eat. The variety of fruits also gives layers of flavour, rather than the single note of lemon, alongside the gentle perfume of rosemary. If you can't get hold of kumquats, just substitute one more lemon.

Serves 4

500g suet pastry, made with shredded vegetable suet (see page 49)

120g butter

2 unwaxed lemons

1 unwaxed orange

3 kumquats

120g caster sugar

Method

Line a baking sheet with parchment paper. Cut off a quarter of the pastry dough and set it aside for the lid. On a lightly floured surface, roll out the other three-quarters of the pastry to a circle slightly less than 1cm thick. Slide the rolled-out pastry onto the lined baking sheet and chill in the fridge for 15 minutes.

Grease the pudding basin with 20g of the butter. Evenly line the pudding basin with the rolled-out pastry, easing it into the basin and being careful to avoid any folds of overlapping dough. Leave any overhanging dough in place around the

Ingredients & method cont. overleaf

100g light brown soft sugar

1 star anise

3 cloves

1 small rosemary sprig, needles picked

To serve

Proper Custard (see page 277), thick double cream or crème fraîche

Equipment

750ml pudding basin

lip of the basin. Pop the basin in the fridge to chill while you roll out the remaining dough to the same thickness as before and to 1cm wider than the basin for the lid. Chill the lid in the fridge with the lined basin.

Using a sharp knife, trim the ends from the citrus fruits and discard them, then cut the fruits into 5mm thick slices, removing any visible pips or seeds. Fill a small pan with water and add the caster sugar. Bring the water up to a simmer and stir to make sure the sugar is fully dissolved. Once the sugar is dissolved, drop the sliced fruits into the pan and simmer for 1 minute. Carefully strain the fruits, discarding the cooking water, and set them aside to cool.

Preheat the oven to 165°C fan/185°C/gas mark 6½.

In a small bowl, combine the remaining butter and brown sugar to form a paste.

Once the fruit slices are cool, arrange them in layers in the lined pudding basin, spreading some of the brown sugar paste evenly throughout the layers and dotting the star anise, whole cloves and rosemary needles amongst the fruit. Do not fill the basin right up to the rim, rather leave a 1cm gap.

Wet the overhanging pastry around the lip of the basin. Lay the pastry lid over the fruit filling, making sure it is centred on the basin. Firmly pinch together the overhanging pastry and the lid, thinning out the dough. Leaving a border of about 1cm, trim away any excess dough using kitchen scissors. Brush that 1cm border with a little water, then fold it back onto the lid of the pudding and flatten it down onto the surface of the pastry.

Cut a circle of parchment paper large enough to cover the surface of the lid and sit it over the top. Next, tear off a sheet of foil measuring 30cm square and fold a 2cm pleat in the centre (this allows for the pudding to expand during steaming). Fit the pleated foil to the top of the basin; it should sit loosely over the surface but fit tightly around the neck. Take a length of string and tightly tie it around the neck of the basin to secure the foil lid in place.

Place the basin in a deep roasting tray. Fill the tray with boiling water so it reaches halfway up the sides of the basin. Tear off another large sheet of foil and use it to seal the roasting tray. Place the tray in the preheated oven and steam the pudding for 3½ hours, topping up the water if the level gets too low.

Once cooked, remove the tray from the oven and the basin from the tray, then rest the pudding for 15 minutes before discarding the foil and parchment paper. Check the pudding is loose around the sides of the basin; if not, run a sharp knife around the inside edge of the bowl. Put a wide, shallow serving dish over the top of the basin and, holding the dish securely in place, quickly flip them both over. Lift off the basin to reveal the pudding.

Serve the pudding with a jug of custard, cream or crème fraîche.

I love
THE IDEA OF THE
whole lemon
AND HOW IT
permeates the pudding,
BUT IT DOES MEAN
that such a large percentage
OF THE
finished dish is inedible.
IT MADE SENSE TO
TACKLE THAT

RÉSERVATIONS UNIQUEMENT
Paris
01 43 72 24 01
18 RU PAUL BERT, 75011

Figgy Pudding

Often considered a precursor to the classic Christmas Plum Pudding, there were recipes for Figgy Pudding in Mrs Beeton's *Book of Household Management*, her cookbook of 1861. Classically made from preserved figs, suet, spices and brown sugar, and then soaked in rum, it would have been a dense, sleep-inducing affair of a dessert.

My version here makes use of the magical properties of baking powder to lighten the sponge whilst retaining the robust flavours of the original. I have used panko breadcrumbs as a modern addition; they bring a lightness to an otherwise quite heavy dish. Panko are double-baked and hold up well in a dish like this instead of immediately turning to stodge! I have also swapped the traditional rum for Amaretto as that gives the same depth of alcohol but adds a nuttiness from its almond flavour. This was probably the recipe I tested the most times for this book. There were many, many failed attempts – some of which I inflicted upon my family (I am so sorry) – before perfecting this pudding, which I think is a joy to eat. Pass the custard, please!

Serves 4–6

15g softened butter, for greasing

100g self-raising flour

2 teaspoons baking powder

80g vegetarian shredded suet

40g ground almonds

50g panko breadcrumbs

Zest of 1 unwaxed lemon

1 teaspoon ground cinnamon

½ teaspoon fine table salt

2 eggs

140g golden caster sugar

150g whole milk

30ml Amaretto liqueur

100g dried figs, stalks removed and cut into small pieces

Method

Preheat the oven to 165°C fan/185°C/gas mark 6½ and lightly grease the savarin mould or bundt tin with the butter.

In a large bowl, combine the flour, baking powder, suet, ground almonds, panko breadcrumbs, lemon zest, ground cinnamon and salt. In a separate bowl, beat the eggs with the sugar until well combined, then whisk in the milk and Amaretto.

Pour the wet ingredients (the egg mixture) into the bowl with the dry ingredients (the flour mixture) and beat together to form a smooth batter. Fold the chopped figs through the batter so they are evenly distributed.

Carefully scrape the batter into the greased mould or tin; the batter should come no more than three-quarters of the way up the sides. Cut out a piece of parchment paper that matches the shape of the mould or tin and sit it over the top. Next, tear off a sheet of foil measuring 50cm square and fold a 2cm pleat in the centre (this allows for the pudding to expand during steaming). Fit the pleated foil to the top of the mould or tin; it should sit loosely over the surface but fit tightly around the sides. Take a length of string and tightly tie it around the sides of the mould or tin to secure the foil lid in place.

Ingredients & method cont. overleaf

To serve

Proper Custard (see page 277)

10g flaked almonds, toasted

Equipment

20cm savarin ring mould or 6-cup fluted bundt tin

Place the mould or tin in a deep roasting tray. Fill the tray with boiling water so it reaches halfway up the sides of the mould or tin. Tear off another large sheet of foil and use it to seal the roasting tray. Place the tray in the preheated oven and steam the pudding for $2\frac{1}{2}$ hours.

Once cooked, remove the tray from the oven and the pudding from the tray, and rest the pudding for 15 minutes before discarding the foil and parchment paper. Check the pudding is loose around the sides of the mould or tin. If necessary, gently prise the pudding away from the sides with a small knife. Turn out the pudding into a wide, shallow bowl.

To serve, pour the custard over the pudding. If you have used a savarin ring mould, fill the cavity at the centre of the pudding and allow a little custard to drizzle down the sides. If you have used a fluted bundt tin, pour the custard over the top of the pudding and allow it to cascade down the grooves. Finish with a scattering of toasted almonds before serving.

Manchester Tart

Recorded in Mrs Beeton's *Book of Household Management* in 1861 as Manchester Pudding, her recipe is for a puff pastry case with a layer of jam and a custard filling. The recipe for what is now known as Manchester Tart seems to have originated in the nineteenth century in that city as a working-class dessert. As such it would have had humble breadcrumbs in the bottom of the dish rather than pastry.

I remember this being served as a tart for a school dinner pudding in the nineties, as it had been since the seventies. It was usually a shortcrust pastry case filled with the familiar jam and custard, but also finished with a sprinkling of desiccated coconut and topped with a preserved cherry (which never tasted of cherry and had its own unique flavour). Here my recipe stays true to that Manchester Tart of my childhood but with a few modern touches to lighten it all.

Serves 6–8

400g sweet shortcrust pastry (see page 38, or shop-bought)

5g softened butter, for greasing

1 egg yolk, strained and beaten, for egg washing

For the filling

800g Pastry Cream (see page 276)

160g raspberry jam

30g desiccated coconut, lightly toasted

To decorate

Around 50g raspberries, cut in half

1 teaspoon freeze-dried raspberries, crumbled

Method

Several hours ahead of time, make the pastry cream and chill in the fridge until needed.

On a lightly floured surface, roll out the pastry dough to a large circle, about 25cm in diameter and just under 5mm thick. Slide the rolled-out pastry onto a parchment-lined baking tray, trim off any excess and chill in the fridge for 20 minutes.

Grease the insides of the tart tin with the butter and then line it with the chilled disc of pastry. To do this, roll the pastry around the rolling pin and lay it carefully over the tin. Press the dough firmly against the sides of the tin and into the corners, making sure it is in contact with the tin. Allow the excess pastry to come up and over the top edge by a few centimetres, then press the overhanging dough against the outside of the tin to secure it in place. Using a fork, prick the base of the pastry case all over. Chill the pastry case in the fridge for 30 minutes.

Preheat the oven to 180°C fan/200°C/gas mark 6.

Line the pastry case with parchment paper and fill with ceramic baking beans right to the top. Place the tin in the preheated oven and bake the pastry case for 20 minutes. Carefully remove the baking beans and parchment paper, then turn the pastry case by 180 degrees in the oven to ensure it cooks evenly. Bake for a further 10 minutes. Finally, lightly brush the surface of the pastry all over with the egg yolk and return to the oven for a further 2 minutes. Set aside to cool.

Ingredients & method cont. overleaf

10 Maraschino cherries, stems removed and cut in half

10–12 small mint leaves

Equipment

20cm round loose-bottomed tart tin

Ceramic baking beans

You can either leave the pastry case untrimmed for a more rustic look, as I have here, or once cooled, using a vegetable peeler, trim the overhanging top edge of the pastry case back to the top of the tin to make a neat edge. Release the pastry case from the tart tin.

Spoon the jam into the pastry case to evenly cover the bottom and then smooth it over with a silicone spatula. Next, scrape the pastry cream into a piping bag. Pipe the pastry cream on top of the jam in a thick layer. Sprinkle the desiccated coconut over the pastry cream until it is fully covered. (If you need to toast the desiccated coconut, place it in a frying pan over a medium heat and keep stirring until it is an even, light brown colour.) Finally, top the tart with the fresh raspberries, freeze-dried raspberries and halved Maraschino cherries, then scatter over the mint leaves.

Serve slices of the tart with a few extra fresh raspberries on the side and a drizzle of single cream.

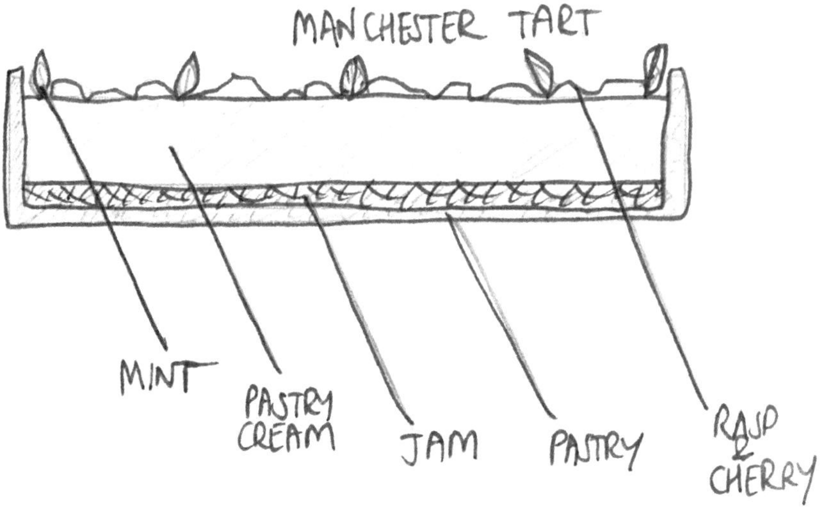

Treacle Tart

From mentions in *Chitty Chitty Bang Bang* to being Harry Potter's favourite food, Treacle Tart has a well-deserved place within fictional worlds as a childhood favourite. If not careful, however, recipes for this pudding can be very sugary; whilst that may appeal to kids with a sweet tooth, it is probably less attractive to adults. Golden syrup is the main ingredient of the Treacle Tart, as we now know it, although the first written recipe in a late nineteenth-century cookbook by Mary Jewry pre-dated the invention of golden syrup. In Jewry's recipe, black treacle takes its place, which would have made for a pretty heavy texture, I think.

In order to keep the filling of this tart as light as possible, I have added panko breadcrumbs and oats to the golden syrup, plus the combination of both orange and lemon zest cuts through the richness and adds a lift of citrus flavour. Treacle Tart is always best eaten just after it has cooled to room temperature, but if you do prefer to eat it warm then allow the tart to cool first before reheating.

Serves 8–10

- 400g sweet shortcrust pastry (see page 38, or shop-bought)
- 5g softened butter, for greasing
- 1 egg yolk, strained and beaten for egg washing

For the filling

- 55g butter
- 50ml double cream
- 400g golden syrup
- Zest of 1 unwaxed orange
- Zest of 1 unwaxed lemon
- Pinch of fine table salt
- 2 eggs, beaten
- 110g panko breadcrumbs
- 40g steel-cut or pinhead oats

Method

On a lightly floured surface, roll out the pastry dough to a large circle, about 25cm in diameter and just under 5mm thick. Slide the rolled-out pastry onto a parchment-lined baking tray, trim off any excess and chill in the fridge for 20 minutes.

Grease the insides of the tart tin with the 5g of butter and then line it with the chilled disc of pastry. To do this, roll the pastry around the rolling pin and lay it carefully over the tin. Press the dough firmly against the sides of the tin and into the corners, making sure it's in contact with the tin. Allow the excess pastry to come up and over the top edge by a few centimetres, then press the overhanging dough against the outside of the tin to secure it in place. Using a fork, prick the base of the pastry case all over. Chill in the fridge for a further 30 minutes.

Preheat the oven to 170°C fan/190°C/gas mark 5.

Line the pastry case with parchment paper and fill with ceramic baking beans right to the top. Place the tin in the preheated oven and bake the pastry case for 20 minutes. Carefully remove the baking beans and parchment paper, then turn the pastry case by 180 degrees in the oven to ensure it cooks evenly. Bake for a further 10 minutes. Finally, brush the pastry case all over with the egg yolk and bake for a final 2 minutes. Set aside to cool.

Ingredients & method cont. overleaf

To serve

Clotted cream or vanilla ice cream

Equipment

20cm round loose-bottomed tart tin

Ceramic baking beans

Lower the oven temperature to 165°C fan/185°C/gas mark 6½.

Put the butter in a medium pan and cook over a medium heat until the buttermilk caramelises – it will look brown and smell nutty. Immediately remove from the heat, add the double cream and golden syrup and mix together thoroughly. Return the pan to the heat and gently warm the syrup mixture through. Remove from the heat and whisk in the citrus zest, salt and beaten eggs.

Combine the panko breadcrumbs and oats in a large bowl. Pour the syrup mixture into the bowl over the breadcrumbs and oats, then fold well together. Pour the filling mixture into the tart case.

Place the tin in the preheated oven and bake the tart for 20 minutes. Turn the tart case by 180 degrees in the oven to ensure it cooks evenly and bake for a further 20 minutes. Remove the tart from the oven and allow to cool to room temperature.

Once cooled, using a vegetable peeler, trim the overhanging top edge of the pastry case back to the top of the tin to make a neat edge. Remove the tart from the tin and place on a large serving plate.

Either serve the tart at room temperature with some clotted cream or warm the slices through in an 180°C fan/200°C/gas mark 6 oven for 10 minutes and serve with scoops of good-quality vanilla ice cream.

Mansfield Pie

In 1927, a 9-kg gooseberry pie was frozen and sent 3,000 miles from Mansfield, just north of Nottingham in the United Kingdom to Mansfield, Massachusetts in the USA. It was sent as a goodwill gift to the namesake American town to celebrate the Mansfield July fair, an annual event in Britain during which gooseberry pies are baked, a tradition that spans back as far as 1377 to celebrate its Market Charter. At the end of the fair, locals would gather to watch the local mayor cut a large gooseberry pie, often filled with almost 30kg of the fruit. The original Mansfield Pie was actually known as a Mansfield Pork Pie, despite never having contained pork, but it was built in the same way as a pork pie using hot-water pastry case that with filled with raw gooseberries and butter before baking. My interpretation of that pie similarly celebrates gooseberries, which are at their best in July, and complements the fruit with some walnut frangipane and crisp pastry.

Serves 6

400g sweet shortcrust pastry (see page 38, or shop-bought)

5g softened butter, for greasing

1 egg yolk, strained and beaten, for egg washing

300g fresh gooseberries, topped and tailed

For the walnut frangipane

150g shelled walnut pieces

150g softened butter

150g light brown soft sugar

1 vanilla pod, split lengthways and seeds scraped

1 large egg, beaten

100g plain flour

Photographed overleaf

Method

On a lightly floured surface, roll out the pastry dough to a circle about 25cm in diameter and just under 5mm thick. Slide the rolled-out pastry onto a parchment-lined baking tray, trim off any excess and chill in the fridge for 20 minutes.

Grease the insides of the tart tin with butter and then line it with the disc of pastry. Press the dough firmly against the sides of the tin and into the corners, making sure it is in contact with the tin. Allow the excess pastry to come up and over the top edge, then press the overhanging dough against the outside of the tin to secure it in place. Using a fork, prick the base of the pastry case all over. Chill the pastry case in the fridge for 30 minutes.

Preheat the oven to 170°C fan/190°C/gas mark 5.

Line the pastry case with parchment paper and fill with ceramic baking beans right to the top. Bake in the hot oven for 20 minutes. Carefully remove the baking beans and parchment paper, then turn the pastry case by 180 degrees in the oven to ensure it cooks evenly and bake for a further 10 minutes. Finally, brush the pastry case all over with the egg yolk and bake for a final 2 minutes.

Meanwhile, make the walnut frangipane. Whizz the walnuts in a food processor until they resemble breadcrumbs.

In a separate bowl, beat together the butter, sugar and vanilla seeds until pale and fluffy. Gradually fold in the beaten eggs until fully incorporated. Next, fold in the flour followed by the ground walnuts.

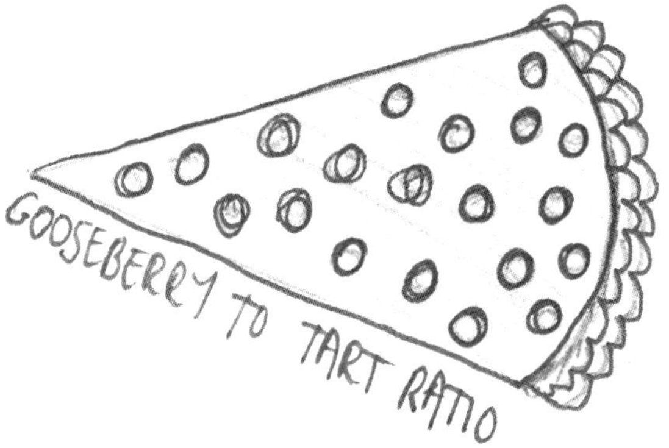

To serve

Clotted cream

Equipment

20cm round loose-bottomed tart tin

Ceramic baking beans

Scrape the walnut frangipane into the tart case and level the surface. Stud the frangipane all over with the gooseberries, pushing them in just halfway.

Lower the oven temperature to 165°C fan/185°C/gas mark 4½.

Place the tin in the preheated oven and bake the pie for 30 minutes or until the frangipane just starts to rise in the centre.

Serve slices of the pie warm with curls of clotted cream and some hot tea.

Banoffee Pie

Nigel Mackenzie and Ian Dowding, I salute you. Nigel (the restaurateur) and Ian (the chef) of The Hungry Monk in Jevington, East Sussex, created this dish together in 1972 while trying to innovate a new dessert menu. Ian recommended a coffee-flavoured pudding that he had eaten in the USA and Nigel suggested the addition of bananas. In that sixteenth-century tearoom, a legend was born. The recipe for Banoffee Pie was printed proudly in their cookbook *The Deeper Secrets of The Hungry Monk*, published in 1974.

Banoffee Pie easily sits in my top ten of worldwide puddings. The caramel, the coffee, the cream, all complementing the bananas. It is a superb creation. I know that Nigel and Ian used shortcrust pastry as the base for their pie, but – please forgive me – I prefer the digestive biscuit base. Here I have made that biscuit base with brown butter and oats for a deeper flavour and texture that enhances the pie further.

The addition of gelatine to the whipped cream gives it structure, so it is nicer to slice after refrigeration. When assembling the pie, do not push the sliced bananas too far into the caramel filling as they will macerate from the sugar and the extra liquid will make it all very loose.

When we have friends around to our home, I like to set the whole banoffee pie down on the table for a bit of wow factor before cutting generous slices for everyone. Guests always say, 'Oh, I'll start with just a small piece,' but they don't really mean it. Give everyone a hearty wedge and make them happy.

Serves 6–8

For the biscuit base

220g digestive biscuits
30g rolled oats
140g butter

For the banoffee filling

2 × 397g tins condensed milk
¼ teaspoon fine table salt
6 medium just-ripe bananas

For the coffee cream topping

1 sheet of bronze gelatine
550ml double cream

Ingredients & method cont. overleaf

Method

Either the day before or first thing on the day of making, remove the labels from the tins of condensed milk and lay them on their sides in a large, deep pan. Fill the pan with plenty of water so the tins are well covered. Bring the water up to a simmer and cook the tins of condensed milk for 2½ hours, topping up the water whenever necessary so the tins are always fully submerged.

Once cooked, carefully remove the tins from the pan and allow to cool in iced water for at least 1 hour, or leave out to cool naturally for at least 4 hours. It is very important to allow the tins to cool completely to avoid them exploding and risking painful burns from scalding hot toffee.

To make the biscuit base, blitz the digestives in a food processor until fine crumbs. Alternatively, crush the biscuits by hand in a bowl or place them in a ziplock bag and bash them with a rolling pin. Place the biscuit crumbs in a bowl with the oats and set aside.

Put the butter in a medium pan and cook over a medium heat until the buttermilk caramelises – it will look brown and smell nutty. Immediately turn off the heat, add the biscuit crumbs and oats and mix together thoroughly.

1 vanilla pod, split lengthways and seeds scraped

1 tablespoon instant coffee

50g icing sugar

To decorate

2 medium just-ripe bananas

100g caster sugar

15g butter

20ml rum

30g shelled pecans

5g cocoa powder, sifted

50g dark chocolate (minimum 70% cocoa)

Equipment

22cm round loose-bottomed tart tin

Line the base of the tart tin with a disc of greaseproof paper. Spoon the biscuit base mixture into the tin and, using the back of the spoon, press the mixture down onto the base and into the sides of the tin to make a firm, even crust. Chill in the fridge for 30 minutes.

When it is safe to do so, open the cooled tins of condensed milk. Add a pinch of salt to each tin and stir through the toffee mixture. Scoop out the salted toffee into the pie case, then spread it evenly over the base. Chill the pie in the fridge for 15 minutes.

For the coffee cream topping, soak the gelatine leaf in cold water until soft. In a pan, combine 100ml of the cream with the seeds scraped from the vanilla pod and the instant coffee. Heat the cream just to hot but not scalding. Squeeze any excess water from the gelatine and whisk it into the hot coffee cream until fully melted. Set aside to cool to room temperature.

Meanwhile, make the caramelised bananas and pecans for the decoration. Peel the 2 bananas and slice them into 3cm rounds. Heat the caster sugar in a dry pan over a medium heat until the sugar melts and turns a light caramel colour. Turn the heat right down, allow the caramel to go a bit darker – almost a mahogany colour – and then add in the butter and rum. Do not stir, instead swirl the pan until everything is well combined. Add the banana slices and pecans, toss them in the caramel until well coated, then remove with a fork and lay on a sheet of parchment paper. To clean the pan, let it cool slightly then fill with water, bring to a boil for a few minutes (with the fork in it too) and then pour the liquid down the sink.

Before adding the bananas and coffee cream topping to the pie, remove the pie case from the tart tin, peel off the parchment paper from the base and sit the pie on a flat serving plate.

Peel the 6 bananas for the filling and slice them into 1cm rounds before neatly covering the surface of the toffee with the banana slices, only pressing on them very lightly.

Once the coffee cream has cooled, whisk it into the remaining cream. Sift over the icing sugar and whisk it into the cream until firm peaks form, although you still want to be able to spoon it onto the pie. Use a flexible silicone spatula to get all the coffee cream from the bowl onto the pie, creating a mountain of cream with rustic peaks.

To decorate, dust the banoffee pie liberally with the cocoa powder and then stud the topping with the caramelised bananas and pecans. Finally, use a vegetable peeler to shave curls of chocolate all over the topping.

Bilberry Pies

Known as blaeberries or wimberries in Scotland, bilberries are small round berries that grow in moorland areas and can be picked during the late summer. They are very dark blue in colour, sometimes almost black, but with pink flesh inside. Similar in appearance to blueberries, they are a little sharper in flavour and juicier in texture. When the berries are in season, bilberry pies can be found in abundance all over Yorkshire. These are often just a simple shortcrust pastry case with a bilberry and sugar filling; however, I find that can be too wet as the cooked bilberries produce so much juice, so my recipe accounts for this by thickening the fruit filling with a little cornflour. I have also tested this recipe using blueberries as a direct replacement for bilberries because of the difficulty in sourcing them. However, if you know where the wild bilberries grow, I implore you to get out there and pick them while you can. A fine British berry.

Serves 4

600g sweet shortcrust pastry (see page 38, or shop-bought)

15g softened butter

1 egg yolk, strained and beaten with 1 teaspoon water, for egg washing

For the filling

400g Pastry Cream (see page 276)

700g fresh bilberries or blueberries

130g caster sugar

Zest of 1 unwaxed lemon

15g cornflour

Equipment

Four 10cm round non-stick tart tins

Ceramic baking beans

Piping bag (optional)

Method cont. overleaf

Method

Several hours ahead of time, make the pastry cream and chill in the fridge until needed.

On a lightly floured surface, roll out the pastry dough to a large square, at least 30cm and about 5mm thick. Slide the rolled-out pastry onto a parchment-lined baking tray and chill in the fridge for 30 minutes.

While the dough is resting, place the berries, sugar and lemon zest in a pan and cook over a medium heat; lightly crush a few of the berries to release a little juice. When the berries have come up to a simmer, remove the pan from the heat and allow to sit for a few minutes.

In a small bowl, mix the cornflour and a few tablespoons of cold water to make a slurry. Stir the cornflour paste into the berry mixture, bring everything back up to a simmer and, stirring continuously, cook for 1 minute and then set aside to cool to room temperature.

Meanwhile, grease the insides of the tart tins with the softened butter. Cut out four 15cm discs from the rolled-out pastry and use them to line the tins. Press the dough firmly against the sides of the tin and into the corners, making sure it's in contact with the tin and not overlapping. I prefer a more rustic look for these tarts, so I leave the top edges of the pastry cases untrimmed. Chill the pastry cases in the fridge for 15 minutes.

Preheat the oven to 180°C fan/200°C/gas mark 6.

Using a fork, prick the bases of the pastry cases all over. Line the pastry cases with circles of parchment paper large enough to reach up the sides of the tins. Fill each tin up to the rim with the ceramic baking beans. Place the tins in the preheated oven and bake the pastry cases for 15 minutes. Carefully remove the baking beans and parchment paper, then turn the pastry cases by 180 degrees in the oven to ensure they cook evenly. Lower the oven temperature to 170°C fan/190°C/gas mark 5 and bake for 10 minutes. Finally, lightly brush the surface of the pastry all over with the egg wash and return to the oven for a further 2 minutes. Remove from the oven and set aside to cool. Once the pie cases have cooled slightly, gently tip them out of their tins and transfer to a wire rack to cool completely.

When the pie cases have cooled to room temperature, fill a piping bag with the pastry cream. Pipe a quarter of the pastry cream into each pie case, then spoon over a generous amount of the berry mixture to fill the pie cases right up to the top. (If you don't have a piping bag, just spoon the pastry cream into the pie cases and top with the berry mixture.)

Serve the pies simply by themselves, but with plenty of napkins for dabbing drippy chins.

ACCOMP-ANIMENTS

Beef & Stout Gravy

A deep and rich gravy that works so well with many of the pies in this book. Cornflour can be used as a substitute for potato starch in equal amounts, but it will leave the sauce with a slightly cloudier finish.

Serves 4–6

20ml vegetable oil

1 large Spanish onion, peeled and thinly sliced

1 teaspoon fine table salt

3 garlic cloves, peeled and crushed

330ml dark stout beer

1 litre beef stock

2 rosemary sprigs

6 thyme sprigs

4 tablespoons potato starch (or cornflour)

Method

In a medium pan, warm the oil over a medium heat for a minute. Add the sliced onion and salt to the pan and cook for 5 minutes, allowing the onions to colour slightly. Add the garlic and cook for a further 5 minutes, stirring occasionally.

Pour in the stout and cook until the liquid has reduced by two-thirds. Add the beef stock, rosemary and thyme and cook until reduced by half. Strain the beef stock through a sieve into a clean pan, discarding the vegetables and herbs.

Mix the potato starch with 2 tablespoons of water in a small bowl to make a slurry. Whisk the slurry into the stock.

Return the pan to the heat and, whisking continuously, bring everything to a simmer until the stock thickens to a gravy consistency. Taste to check the seasoning, adjusting as needed.

Photographed on page 181

Mint & Caper Sauce

A piquant sauce that lifts a Katt Pie (see page 202).

Serves 4–6

100ml malt vinegar

40g caster sugar

1 banana shallot, peeled and finely chopped

50g mint leaves, finely chopped

Pinch of fine table salt

15g capers

Method

Place the vinegar and sugar in a small pan with the shallot. Bring to the boil, then add the mint with a pinch of fine table salt and cook for 30 seconds. Fold in the capers. Transfer to a bowl and chill in the fridge until needed.

Serve cold.

Photographed on page 253

Green Herb Sauce

One of my all-time favourite dressings. It's bright and vibrant, and while it sits perfectly alongside a Butter Pie (see page 52) or Welsh Oggie (see page 206), it can also be served with some grilled fish or chicken.

Makes 500ml

2 bunches flat-leaf parsley
1 bunch curly parsley
2 bunches basil
2 bunches mint
100g capers
40ml sherry vinegar
40ml Dijon mustard
400ml extra virgin olive oil
Pinch of fine table salt

Method

Pick the leaves from all the herbs.

Add the capers, vinegar and mustard to a blender and gently pulse until smooth.

Add half of the oil and half of the picked herbs, then blend again until smooth.

Add a good pinch of fine table salt, then the remaining picked herbs and the rest of the oil. Blend again until just smooth.

Any leftover sauce can be stored in the freezer for up to 2 months.

Photographed on page 207

Spinach & Nutmeg Sauce

An earthy green sauce that works well as a balance to the savoury Rasher Pudding (see page 152).

Serves 4

50g butter

1 Spanish onion, peeled and finely chopped

1 teaspoon fine table salt

1 garlic clove, peeled and minced

½ whole nutmeg

100ml double cream

500g baby spinach, washed

Juice of ½ lemon

Method

Melt the butter in a heavy-based pan (large enough to hold all the spinach) over a medium heat. Add the onion and salt and cook until the onion has just softened. Add the garlic and cook for another few minutes, then finely grate in the nutmeg.

Pour in the double cream and cook until it has reduced by half. Add the spinach, pop the lid on the pan and let the spinach wilt for a minute before lifting the lid and stirring. Add 100ml of water, bring the liquid to a simmer and cook, stirring continuously, for 3 minutes.

Transfer everything to a blender (or use a handheld stick blender) and blend until you have a smooth sauce. Finish by stirring the lemon juice through the sauce to taste.

Photographed on page 153

Spiced Brown Ketchup

This is a deeply layered, umami-rich sauce that you will be licking off the back of a spoon. It is superb with cold meat pies and works best, I think, with the Gala Pie (see page 132).

Makes 400g

- 2 × 400g tins chopped tomatoes
- 1 large Spanish onion, peeled and roughly chopped
- 1 Bramley apple, peeled, cored and diced
- 50g pitted medjool dates
- 100g dark soft brown sugar
- 1 tablespoon black treacle
- 100ml red wine vinegar
- 1 tablespoon Worcestershire sauce
- 2 teaspoons mustard powder
- 3 teaspoons ground ginger
- 3 teaspoons ground cinnamon
- 1 teaspoon ground white pepper
- ½ teaspoon ground cloves
- 1 teaspoon fine table salt

Method

Put all the ingredients in a large, heavy-based pan and add 500ml of water. Bring to a simmer over a low heat and cook until almost all the liquid has evaporated.

Transfer everything to a blender (or use a handheld stick blender) and blend until you have a smooth sauce.

When stored in an airtight container in the fridge, this sauce will keep for up to 2 weeks.

Photographed on page 193

Spicy Green Chutney

A fresh yet heady dressing that is so easy to make. It complements the Balti Pie superbly (see page 106).

Makes 150ml

1 garlic clove, peeled

2cm piece ginger, peeled

1 green chilli

½ teaspoon cumin seeds, lightly toasted

Juice of ½ lemon

60g coriander, leaves picked

40g mint, leaves picked

Pinch of fine table salt

Method

In a blender, blitz together the garlic, ginger, chilli, cumin seeds, lemon juice and 4 tablespoons of water until smooth. Add the coriander and mint leaves with a pinch of salt and blend again until smooth.

When stored in an airtight container in the fridge, this chutney will keep for up to 1 week.

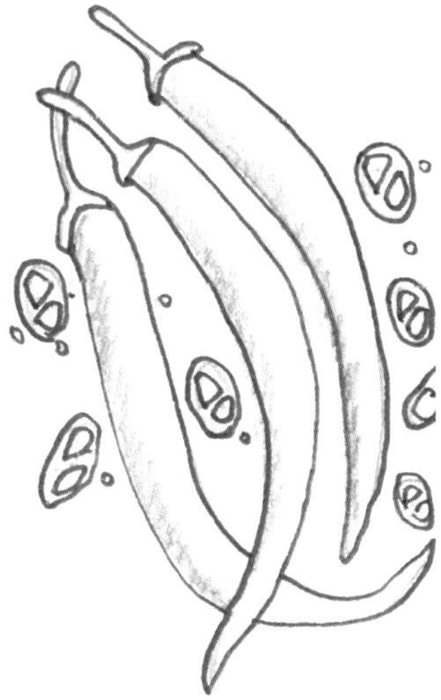

Photographed on page 109

Dill & Turmeric Pickled Eggs

These brightly coloured, piquant eggs converted me into a fan of the pickled egg. These make for a lovely lunch alongside a warm Homity Pie (see page 56).

Makes 6

6 medium free-range eggs
250ml apple cider vinegar
50g caster sugar
30g fresh turmeric
1 teaspoon English mustard powder
1 teaspoon brown mustard seeds
½ bunch dill

Method

Bring a large pan of water to a simmer over a medium heat. Carefully lower the eggs into the simmering water with a spoon, making sure you don't crack them on the base of the pan, and cook for 7 minutes.

Meanwhile, fill a large bowl with iced water and keep it close by. Remove the eggs from the pan using a slotted spoon and plunge them into the iced water to stop them cooking any further. Leave the eggs to cool for at least 10 minutes. Once cool enough to handle, carefully peel the shells from the eggs. Re-fill the bowl with fresh water, then leave the peeled eggs in the water until needed.

In the same pan, bring the vinegar, sugar, turmeric, mustard powder and mustard seeds to a simmer over a medium heat. Remove from the heat and allow to cool to room temperature.

Meanwhile, sterilise a large preserving jar by submerging it in a pan of simmering water for at least 10 minutes.

Pour the vinegar mixture into the sterilised jar. Carefully drop the boiled eggs into the jar along with the dill and seal with the lid. Leave the eggs to pickle for at least a few days before using. They are best eaten after 1 week. When stored in a sealed jar in the fridge, these pickled eggs will keep for up to 1 month.

Spiced Tomato Chutney

A rich, heady alternative to ketchup that is totally delicious. It adds a level of complexity to the Macaroni Pie (see page 62).

Makes 500ml

1 teaspoon nigella seeds

500g red onions, peeled and thinly sliced)

500g plum tomatoes, roughly chopped

1 garlic clove, peeled and finely chopped

10g ginger, peeled and finely chopped

120g dark brown sugar

75ml red wine vinegar

Method

Preheat the oven to 180°C fan/200°C/gas mark 6.

Toast the nigella seeds in the preheated oven for 5 minutes. (This can also be done in a dry pan over a medium heat, if you want to avoid putting the oven on just for this.)

Place the toasted nigella seeds along with all the other ingredients in a heavy-based pan. Bring to a simmer and cook until the mixture becomes jammy and takes on a chutney consistency. Remove from the heat and leave to cool.

Meanwhile, sterilise a 500ml jar by submerging it in a pan of simmering water for at least 10 minutes.

Fill the sterilised jar with the chutney and seal with the lid. When stored in a sealed jar in the fridge, this chutney will keep for up to 1 month.

Photographed on page 63

Beer-Pickled Baby Onions

A classic British pub snack; its acidity lends itself perfectly to a Pork Pie (see page 122).

Fills a 1-litre jar

200g baby silverskin onions, peeled
300ml bitter beer
200ml white wine vinegar
40g demerara sugar
60g clear honey
5 juniper berries
10 thyme sprigs

Method

Place the onions in a small pan, pour in the beer and bring to a simmer over a medium heat. Add the vinegar, sugar, honey, juniper berries and thyme sprigs to the pan and bring everything back to a simmer. Remove from the heat and allow to cool.

Meanwhile, sterilise a large preserving jar by submerging it in a pan of simmering water for at least 10 minutes.

Pour the pickled onions and liquid into the sterilised jar and seal with the lid. When stored in a sealed jar in the fridge, these pickled onions will keep for up to 3 months.

Photographed on page 253

Chunky Piccalilli

Another British condiment classic. This works with almost all of the cold pies in this book, but I think it is best paired with the Gala Pie (see page 132), cutting through the richness of the pork and egg.

Fills a 1-litre jar

200g baby silverskin onions

1 small cauliflower, cut into small florets

1 red pepper, deseeded and cut into 2cm dice

500ml malt vinegar

80g caster sugar

1 large cucumber, deseeded and cut into 2cm dice

100g French beans, cut into 2cm lengths

2 garlic cloves, peeled and thinly sliced

1 heaped tablespoon English mustard powder

2 teaspoons ground turmeric

½ teaspoon ground allspice

1 tablespoon plain flour

1 teaspoon cornflour

Method

Place the onions, cauliflower and red pepper in a medium pan, pour in the vinegar, stir in the sugar and bring to a gentle simmer over a medium heat for 3 minutes. Add in the cucumber, French beans and garlic, then cook for a further minute.

Tip the contents of the pan into a colander set over a large jug or bowl. Allow the vinegar mixture to strain off into the jug. Set aside the vegetables.

Combine the mustard powder, turmeric, allspice, plain flour and cornflour in a small bowl, add a few tablespoons of the reserved vinegar mixture and stir to make a slurry.

Pour the rest of the vinegar mixture back into the pan, stir in the slurry and bring to a simmer over a medium heat, whisking continuously until smooth. Return the vegetables to the pan.

Meanwhile, sterilise a large preserving jar by submerging it in a pan of simmering water for at least 10 minutes.

Fill the sterilised jar with the piccalilli and seal with the lid. When stored in a sealed jar in the fridge, this piccalilli will keep for up to 2 months.

Photographed on page 253

Braised Red Cabbage

A lovely wintery side dish. The depth of the spices makes it an ideal accompaniment to the Yorkshire Christmas Pie (see page 98).

Serves 8

- 50g butter
- 1 red onion, peeled and thinly sliced
- ½ red cabbage, core removed and leaves thinly sliced
- 1 teaspoon fine table salt
- 1 star anise
- ½ cinnamon stick
- 1 tablespoon honey
- 300ml orange juice
- 3 tarragon sprigs, leaves picked and chopped, plus a few whole leaves to garnish

Method

In a wide-based pan, melt the butter over a medium heat. Add the red onion and cook for a few minutes until softened. Add the red cabbage and salt and cook for a further few minutes to soften. Add the star anise and cinnamon stick, drizzle in the honey, pour over the orange juice and simmer over a medium heat for about 1 hour or until the liquid has almost evaporated and the red cabbage is glossy.

When ready to serve, remove the star anise and cinnamon stick, then fold through the tarragon leaves. Garnish with a few more whole tarragon leaves.

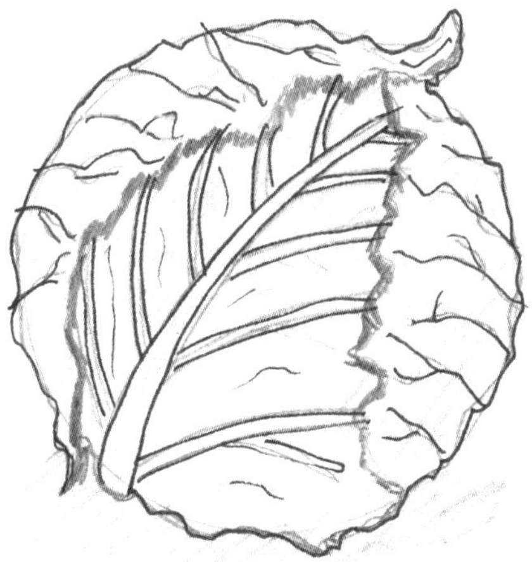

Garlic Breadcrumbs

A perfect savoury topping that can be sprinkled over bowls of pasta or used as the breading for a Scotch egg. Here, it works brilliantly as the finishing touch on a Macaroni Pie (see page 62).

Makes 220g

4 garlic cloves (in their skins)

2 sprigs of thyme (leaves picked and stems discarded)

100g butter

120g panko breadcrumbs

Zest of 1 unwaxed lemon

¼ teaspoon fine table salt

Method

Lightly crush the garlic cloves and add them to a wide frying pan along with the butter and the thyme leaves. Melt the butter over a medium heat until just bubbling, then tip in the panko breadcrumbs.

Toss everything well in the butter and continue to cook for a few minutes until the breadcrumbs turn golden. Season with the lemon zest and salt.

Set aside to cool (with the garlic cloves) before using as directed in the recipe.

Any leftovers can be stored in an airtight container for up to 1 week.

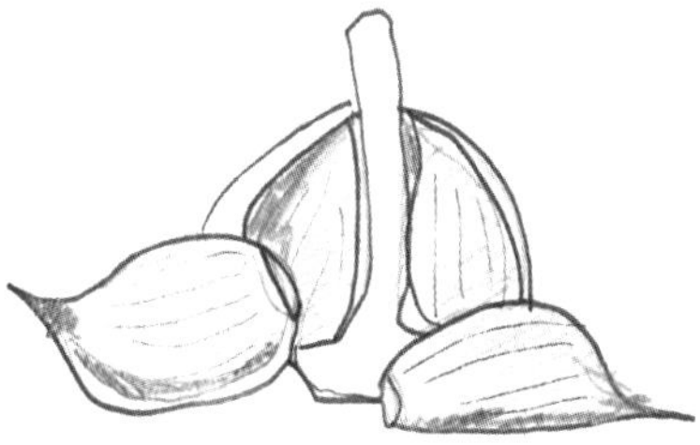

Tomato, Red Onion & Sherry Vinegar Salad

Lovely on a summer's day, this salad is all about simplicity and good ingredients. Try to pick out some absolutely cracking tomatoes to go into this dish and serve it with the Herb Pie (see page 76) for a great lunch.

Serves 4

500g mixed heritage tomatoes

250g baby plum tomatoes

2 red onions, peeled and thinly sliced

30ml sherry vinegar

50ml cold-pressed rapeseed oil

1 teaspoon sea salt

¼ bunch flat-leaf parsley, leaves picked

Method

If stored in the fridge, allow the tomatoes to come up to room temperature.

In a large bowl, marinate the sliced red onions in the sherry vinegar and oil with the sea salt for 5 minutes.

Meanwhile, cut the tomatoes into halves or quarters depending on their size.

Toss the tomatoes through the marinated red onions and fold in the parsley leaves. Serve immediately.

Pickled Beetroot, Apple & Mint Salad

This bright, crisp salad is good all year round on the family table. Its acidity cuts through cheesy dishes and is a great balance for the Likky Pie (see page 68).

Serves 4

300g cooked red beetroot

450ml jar pickled red beetroot, drained

2 Pink Lady apples. peeled and cored

4 mint sprigs, leaves picked

For the dressing

60ml extra virgin olive oil

30ml apple cider vinegar

1 teaspoon Dijon mustard

1 teaspoon clear honey

Coarse sea salt flakes

Method

First, make the dressing. Whisk together the oil, vinegar, mustard and honey with a few pinches of flaky sea salt.

Cut all the beetroot and apples into thick wedges, then toss in the dressing.

Arrange the salad over a serving platter, then roughly tear the mint leaves and scatter across the top of the salad.

Buttermilk Mash

I am sharing my recipe here to make the most buttery mash with the perfect ratio of potato to the other ingredients. The buttermilk brings a welcome touch of acidity to balance the creaminess.

Serves 4

1kg floury potatoes (preferably Maris Piper or Desiree)

80ml milk

40ml double cream

80g butter

1 teaspoon fine table salt

½ teaspoon ground white pepper

40ml buttermilk

Method

Peel the potatoes and cut them into quarters. Rinse well under cold water for 1 minute to remove some of the excess starch. Place the potatoes in a large saucepan and cover with plenty of water. Bring to a boil, then lower to a simmer over a medium heat and cook until a small knife easily pierces the centre of the potato without any resistance, around 12–15 minutes.

Drain the potatoes in a colander and steam for at least 5 minutes. Tip the potatoes back into the pan and either pass them through a potato ricer or use a potato masher.

In a separate pan, warm the milk and cream, then pour it into the large pan and stir through the mashed potato. Return the mashed potato to a low heat, fold in the butter and season with the salt and white pepper. Finally, fold the buttermilk through the mash and check that it is warm throughout before serving.

IT IS SO

GOOD

that it

could almost be

served

by itself.

Creamed Leeks

This leek dish makes a tasty partner when paired with any of the pies in this book, but it is so good that it could almost be served by itself.

Serves 4

- 4 leeks, trimmed of the top 3–4cm of green, and washed
- 20ml olive oil
- 50g butter
- 1 teaspoon fine table salt
- 1 tablespoon plain flour
- 200ml double cream
- 1 teaspoon Dijon mustard
- 60g Gruyère cheese, grated
- 30g hazelnuts, lightly toasted and crushed

Method

Preheat the oven to 180°C fan/200°C/gas mark 6.

Cut two of the leeks into 4-cm lengths. Stack them together, cut ends facing upwards, in a small ovenproof dish and drizzle with the olive oil. Bake in the preheated oven for 40 minutes.

While those leeks are roasting, melt the butter in a medium pan. Thinly slice the remaining leeks and add them to the melted butter, stirring for 1 minute. Add the salt and flour, then cook for a further 1 minute, stirring continuously. Next, stir in the cream and mustard and bring everything to a simmer. Remove the pan from the heat and fold in the grated cheese.

Pour the creamy leek mixture into the ovenproof dish, in and around the gaps between the roasted upright leeks. Scatter over the crushed hazelnuts immediately before serving.

Photographed on page 267

Pease Pudding

A dish strongly associated with the North East of England. It is commonly eaten with ham and pork dishes, and it is so, so tasty served hot with a meat pie.

Serves 4

50g butter

1 large Spanish onion, peeled and finely chopped

1 bay leaf

450g yellow split peas

100g Maris Piper potatoes, peeled and diced

1 teaspoon fine table salt

20ml apple cider vinegar

2 rosemary sprigs

Method

In a medium pan, melt 20g of the butter over a medium heat. Add the onion and bay leaf and cook for 3–4 minutes until just softened.

Add the split peas and potatoes to the pan, cover with water and simmer for about 1 hour or until the split peas are starting to break down. If necessary, top up the water during cooking.

Remove and discard the bay leaf. Stir in the salt and vinegar, then cook for another minute. Ladle half of the split pea mixture into a food processor and blend for 1 minute until smooth. Return to the pan with the rest of the split pea mixture and mix well.

When ready to serve, melt the remaining butter in a small pan, add the rosemary and cook until the butter just starts to brown. Remove and discard the rosemary.

Spoon the pease pudding into a serving bowl, then drizzle over the brown butter.

Photographed on page 273

Lancashire Peas

Slow-cooked black peas, taken to the point where they are almost mushy, are fragrant with vegetables and herbs. This is one of my all-time favourite sides and works so well with a Shepherd's Pie (see page 199).

Serves 4

250g carlin peas (dried)

1 teaspoon bicarbonate of soda

30g butter

1 Spanish onion, peeled and finely diced

2 celery sticks, peeled and thinly sliced

1 carrot, peeled and coarsely grated

2 bay leaves

3 thyme sprigs

20ml malt vinegar

1 teaspoon fine table salt

¼ teaspoon freshly ground black pepper

Method

Place the carlin peas in a bowl, cover with cold water, stir in the bicarbonate of soda and leave to soak overnight.

Melt the butter in a large, heavy-based pan over a medium heat, add the onion and celery and sweat down until soft. Add the carrot, bay leaves and thyme.

Drain the soaked carlin peas and tip them into the pan with the vegetables. Pour in enough water to cover the peas, bring to a simmer over a medium heat and cook until the peas start to break down. If necessary, top up the water during cooking.

Remove and discard the bay leaves. Ladle one-third of the carlin pea mixture into a food processor and blend until smooth. Return to the pan with the rest of the pea mixture and mix well. Stir in the vinegar, salt and pepper, then serve.

Photographed on page 273

Mushy Peas

A staple on the football terraces of Britain, this dish is often served alongside a hot pie and gravy, but it is just as delicious with fish and chips.

Serves 4–6

- 2 × 300g tins marrowfat peas
- 40g butter
- 2 banana shallots, peeled and finely chopped
- 1 garlic clove, peeled and chopped
- 20ml sherry vinegar
- Zest and juice of 1 unwaxed lemon
- Fine table salt
- Pinch of ground white pepper

Method

Drain the marrowfat peas, reserving one-quarter of the liquid.

Melt the butter in a medium pan over a medium heat. Add the shallots with a pinch of fine table salt and cook until softened, around 3–4 minutes. Add the garlic and cook for another minute, stirring continuously so the garlic doesn't burn.

Tip the marrowfat peas into the pan, pour in 200ml of water and the sherry vinegar, then gently simmer until the peas start to break down, 30–40 minutes. Finally, add in the reserved liquid from the drained peas, the lemon zest and juice and season with 1 teaspoon of fine table salt and a good pinch of ground white pepper.

Photographed on page 272

Roasted Cauliflower Cheese

Roasting the cauliflower to a deep caramelised colour adds tonnes of flavour into this dish. Make it once and you will not look back; it will doubtless have you roasting cauliflower forever more.

Serves 4

1 medium cauliflower, leaves removed
1 tablespoon vegetable oil
50g butter
45g plain flour
350ml semi-skimmed milk
100g mature Cheddar, grated
1 tablespoon English mustard
30g mozzarella, grated
5g garlic breadcrumbs (see page 258)
Fine table salt and freshly ground black pepper

Method

Preheat the oven to 185°C fan/205°C/gas mark 6. Line a roasting tray with parchment paper or foil.

Rub the cauliflower all over with the vegetable oil, then season with salt and pepper. Sit the cauliflower in the lined tray and roast in the preheated oven for 45 minutes.

While the cauliflower is roasting, make the sauce. Melt the butter in a pan over a low heat, stir in the flour and cook, stirring continuously, for a few minutes until just starting to brown. In a separate pan, warm the milk. Add half of the warmed milk to the roux and cook, stirring continuously, until lump-free and thickened. Repeat with the remaining milk to make a smooth sauce.

Fold the grated Cheddar and mustard into the sauce and mix until well combined. Take off the heat and gently fold in the mozzarella – do not try to make it smooth!

Turn up the oven temperature to 200°C fan/220°C/gas mark 7.

Place the roasted cauliflower in an ovenproof dish and smother with the sauce. Bake in the hot oven for 10 minutes until just browned. Finally, scatter the garlic breadcrumbs over the cauliflower immediately before serving.

Photographed on page 190

Calvados Cream

This Calvados cream beautifully complements my Apple Pie (see page 216), with the sharp apple brandy cutting through the richness of the crème fraîche.

Makes 200ml

200ml full-fat crème fraîche
20ml Calvados
10g icing sugar, sifted
Zest of 1 unwaxed lemon

Method

Place the crème fraîche in a bowl and fold through the Calvados, icing sugar and lemon zest. Chill in the fridge until just before serving.

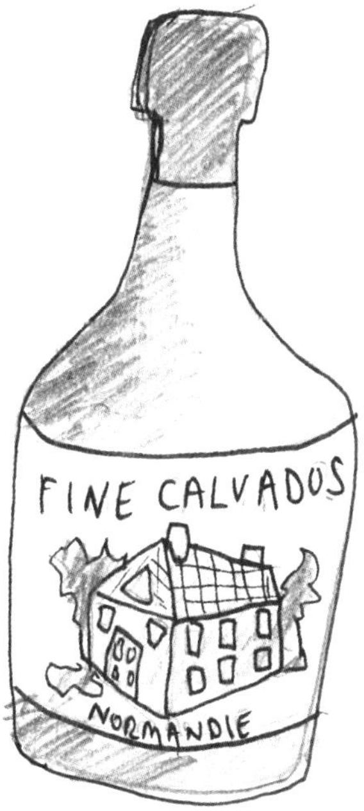

Photographed on page 217

Pastry Cream

A fancier version of custard with a little more structure; because it holds firmer, it is perfect in a tart.

Makes 800ml

480ml whole milk
1 vanilla pod
6 large egg yolks
140g caster sugar
60g cornflour
15g cold butter, cubed

Method

Pour the milk into a small pan. Split open the vanilla pod lengthways and scrape the seeds into the milk, then drop in the empty pod. Warm the milk over a medium heat to a gentle simmer, then remove the pan from the heat. Leave to infuse for 5 minutes.

In a heatproof bowl, whisk together the egg yolks, sugar and cornflour until smooth with no lumps. Remove and discard the vanilla pod from the milk. While whisking continuously, trickle a little of the infused milk into the bowl. Continue whisking until all the milk has been incorporated. Now, gradually pour in the rest of the milk while still whisking.

Return the mixture to the pan and, whisking continuously to stop lumps forming, gently warm it over a low heat until it thickens and a few bubbles just start to break the surface. Remove the pan from the heat and allow to cool for a minute.

Add the cold butter to the pan, whisking until it is fully incorporated and the pastry cream is smooth and glossy.

Transfer the pastry cream to a wide, shallow bowl and cover with clingfilm, pressing it directly onto the surface to stop a skin forming as it cools. Leave to cool fully and then chill in the fridge for at least 3 hours before using.

If piping the pastry cream, whisk to break up the set custard. Continue whisking until the mixture is smooth before transferring the pastry cream to a piping bag.

Proper Custard

A dream combo when poured over a slice of Apple Pie (see page 216). The sweetness of this custard works so well with the tartness of the apple and savouriness of the Cheddar shortcrust pastry.

Serves 4

300ml whole milk
300ml double cream
1 vanilla pod
4 medium egg yolks
35g caster sugar
2 teaspoons cornflour

Method

Pour the milk and cream into a small pan. Split the vanilla pod lengthways and scrape the seeds from the pod into the pan. Bring the milk and cream to a gentle simmer, stirring frequently to stop it catching on the bottom of the pan, then turn off the heat and allow to infuse for a minute.

Meanwhile, whisk together the egg yolks, sugar and cornflour in a heatproof bowl. Once the milk and cream have been infused, discard the vanilla pod.

Very slowly pour the hot milk and cream mixture into the bowl over the egg yolks, whisking continuously to make a smooth custard.

Transfer the custard from the bowl back into the pan and place over a gentle heat. Bring the custard back up to heat while whisking until the custard thickens (it should be thick enough to coat the back of a spoon), then serve immediately.

Photographed on page 227

Index

D

E

M

N

O

P

Q

R

S

T

V

W

Y

Conversion Tables

WEIGHTS

Metric	Imperial
15g	½oz
20g	¾oz
30g	1oz
55g	2oz
85g	3oz
110g	4oz / ¼lb
140g	5oz
170g	6oz
200g	7oz
225g	8oz / ½lb
255g	9oz
285g	10oz
310g	11oz
340g	12oz / ¾lb
370g	13oz
400g	14oz
425g	15oz
450g	6oz / 1lb
1kg	2lb 4oz
1.5kg	3lb 5oz

LIQUIDS

Metric	Imperial
5ml	1 teaspoon
15ml	1 tablespoon or ½fl oz
30ml	2 tablespoons or 1fl oz
150ml	¼ pint or 5fl oz
290ml	½ pint or 10fl oz
425ml	¾ pint or 16fl oz
570ml	1 pint or 20fl oz
1 litre	1¾ pints
1.2 litres	2 pints

LENGTH

Metric	Imperial
5mm	¼ in
1cm	½ in
2cm	¾ in
2.5cm	1in
5cm	2in
10cm	4in
15cm	6in
20cm	8in
30cm	12in

OVEN TEMPERATURES

°C	°C Fan	Gas Mark	°F
110°C	90°C Fan	Gas Mark ¼	225°F
120°C	100°C Fan	Gas Mark ½	250°F
140°C	120°C Fan	Gas Mark 1	275°F
150°C	130°C Fan	Gas Mark 2	300°F
160°C	140°C Fan	Gas Mark 3	325°F
180°C	160°C Fan	Gas Mark 4	350°F
190°C	170°C Fan	Gas Mark 5	375°F
200°C	180°C Fan	Gas Mark 6	400°F
220°C	200°C Fan	Gas Mark 7	425°F
230°C	210°C Fan	Gas Mark 8	450°F
240°C	220°C Fan	Gas Mark 9	475°F

USEFUL CONVERSIONS

1 tablespoon	3 teaspoons
1 level tablespoon	approx. 15g or ½oz
1 heaped tablespoon	approx. 30g or 1oz
1 egg	55ml / 55g / 1fl oz

About the Author

Through skill, creativity and craft, Calum Franklin has elevated British pie making into an art form. A self-confessed pastry deviant, he has been dubbed London's King of Pies. His love for savoury pastry knows no bounds and he brings his passion to life both in his award-winning restaurants and in his cookbooks.

Drawing on a wealth of culinary experience, Calum worked at a variety of renowned restaurants including The Ivy, Chapter One and Aurora, prior to opening Holborn Dining Room in 2014 and The Pie Room in 2018.

In 2024 Calum expanded his culinary footprint internationally with the opening of Public House, a British Brasserie in the heart of Paris, and later that year relaunched The Georgian, the flagship restaurant of the iconic London department store, Harrods.

In late 2025 Calum and his partners Paul Shearing and Hervé Deville formed the bespoke pie company, The House of Pies, with the aim of elevating pie culture across the UK's retail market.

Calum's bestselling debut cookbook, *The Pie Room*, was published in 2020. *The Modern Pie Maker* is his second book. He is a judge for The British Pie Awards, and in in 2024 was inducted as an honouree member of the Confrérie du Pâté-Croûte.

@chefcalum

Thanks

I have spent time talking to, leaning on and annoying some incredible people along this journey. Ivan Day was one of the first. For years I have danced around contacting Ivan, who I think is probably one of the most esteemed British food historians around. This project finally gave me the first solid reason to reach out to him, but I was nervous. This man is a heavyweight in food history and academia. The courses he has given that I have tried to attend have always been sold out. I was convinced he would not want to talk to me, but happily he agreed. After a few messages, we set up a quick call. And then we talked for hours. In fact, an early afternoon call went through until the sun had gone down. He gave me book lists. People to contact. The places to look. Just an incredible, generous and inspiring man. Thank you, Ivan, your chat energised me and made me excited about British food in a way I had not really been before.

Polly Russell, the food historian and curator at the British Library, is someone I have known since the early days of The Pie Room. We have worked on projects together, filmed TV shows and I once watched her catch a live pigeon whilst at the top of a ladder in the midst of a political protest (a story for another book). She has always been so generous with her time for me and has always been my key to unlocking the riches of the British Library. Thank you for all you did to help me bring this together, Polly.

To my friend John Carey, whose beautiful photography once again graces the pages of a cookbook of mine. I was very lucky to work with John in the early days of Holborn Dining Room and to find someone whose photography complements my work so well. He is an artist of the highest calibre and a joy to gossip with, to talk football with and to sit in traffic with. Thank you, mister.

To Rachel Vere, thank you for your incredible styling on the shoots, for pretending to like my music, for your patience with my pastry fiddling. You have given a sense of place to the book that grounds it and make it feel familiar and exciting at the same time; you are the best.

To the brilliant team at Bloomsbury: Emily North, Rose Brown, Rowan Yapp and Lisa Pendreigh, thank you for your patience, for your feedback and your unwavering enthusiasm for the book. It is a joy to work with you all and to make this our second project together.

To Dave Brown, thank you for your vision with the design and layout on the book. I had been a fan from afar of your previous work and it so was a blessing to get to work with you on something so important to me.

And finally, to my wife Shenali. As always, you are my biggest supporter and cheerleader. You have taught me how to accept criticism, absorb it and to turn it into something positive. Love, always.

BLOOMSBURY ABSOLUTE
Bloomsbury Publishing Plc
50 Bedford Square, London, WC1B 3DP, UK
Bloomsbury Publishing Ireland Ltd,
29 Earlsfort Terrace, Dublin 2, DO2 AY28, Ireland

First published in Great Britain, 2026

A catalogue record for this book is available from the British Library

Library of Congress Cataloguing-in-Publication data has been applied for

ISBN: HB: 978-1-5266-7670-2;
eBook: 978-1-5266-7671-9

10 9 8 7 6 5 4 3 2 1

Publisher Director: Rowan Yapp
Project Editors: Rose Brown and Emily North
Copyeditor: Lisa Pendreigh
Designer: Ape Inc
Photographer: John Carey
Food Stylist: Calum Franklin, with Louise Kennedy and Tim Schilling
Prop Stylist: Rachel Vere
Production: Laura Brodie

Printed in China by C&C Offset Printing Ltd

MIX
Paper | Supporting responsible forestry
FSC www.fsc.org FSC® C008047

To find out more about our authors and books visit www.bloomsbury.com and sign up for our newsletters.

For product-safety related questions contact productsafety@bloomsbury.com

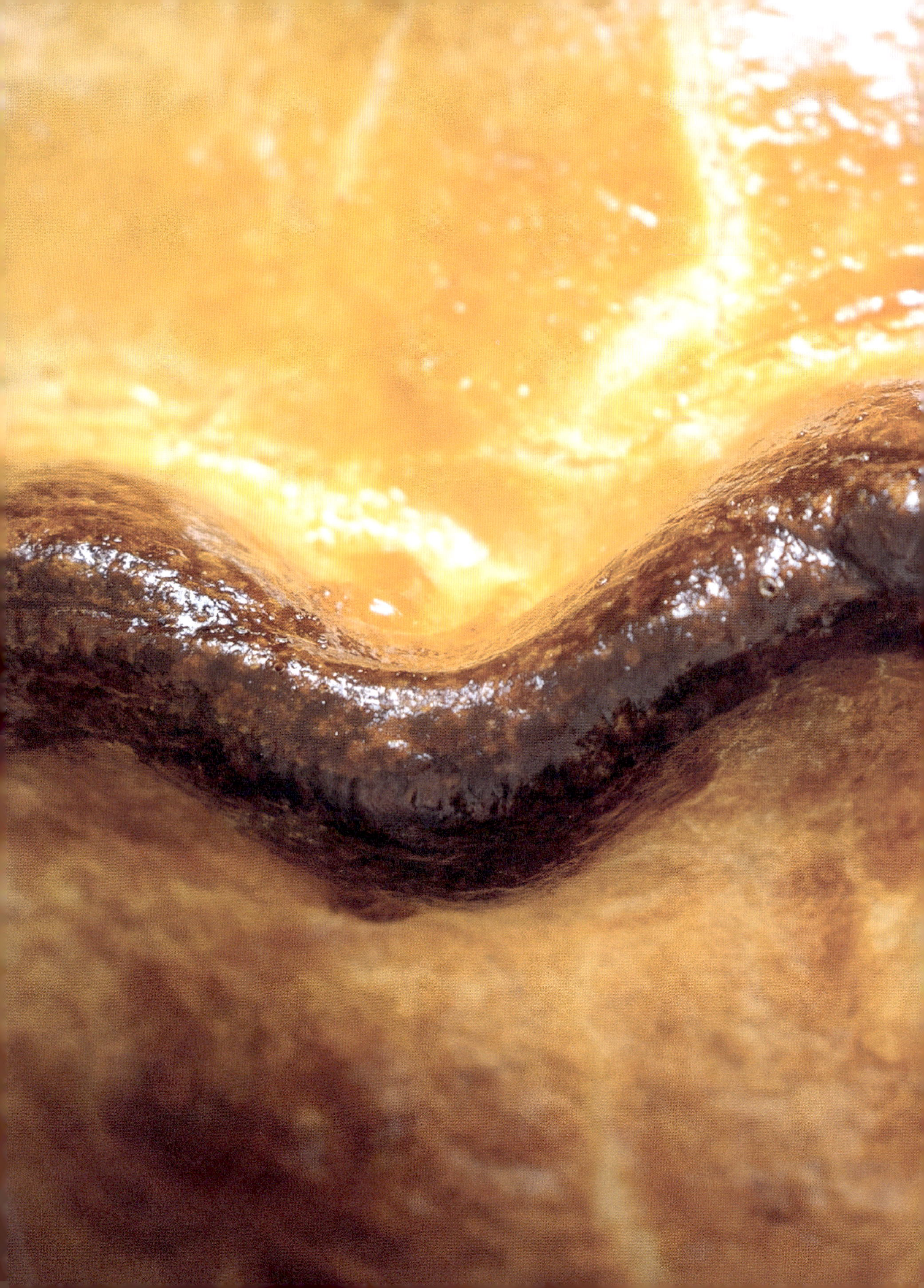